"For the first time I have a comprehensive and practical resource to guide my understanding of my son's experience with executive function as a child with autism. Paula Moraine's work offers powerful insight and readily applicable concepts to empower all parents, teachers, care givers, and professionals as they embrace someone living with ASD. The book's concept of Autistic Access Points has unlocked countless barriers for my child making it possible for him to establish, build, and maintain effective executive skills. Paula Moraine's new paradigm gave me the capability to emphasize his strengths and build upon his talents opening infinite possibilities I could not imagine before reading this book."

—*Michelle Shramek, educator and parent of a child with Autism Spectrum Disorder*

"The descriptions of thinking from an individual with autism are excellent; I felt like I was talking to my patients. They give the reader a unique insight into the way of thinking of a person with an autistic spectrum disorder, allowing them to dispel any misconceptions they may have. The information in this book is clear, well-organised and offers practical solutions to common problems in the autism population."

—*Eric Q. Tridas, Director and Developmental Pediatrician, The Tridas Center for Child Development, Florida*

by the same author

Helping Students Take Control of Everyday Executive Functions
The Attention Fix
Paula Moraine
ISBN 978 1 84905 884 1
eISBN 978 0 85700 576 2

of related interest

Executive Function "Dysfunction"– Strategies
for Educators and Parents
Rebecca A. Moyes, M.Ed.
ISBN 978 1 84905 753 0
eISBN 978 1 78450 045 0

Autism and the Stress Effect
A 4-step lifestyle approach to transform your
child's health, happiness, and vitality
Theresa Hamlin
Foreword by John Ratey and Temple Grandin
ISBN 978 1 84905 748 6
eISBN 978 1 78450 178 5

AUTISM
AND
EVERYDAY EXECUTIVE FUNCTION

A STRENGTHS-BASED APPROACH FOR IMPROVING ATTENTION, MEMORY, ORGANIZATION, AND FLEXIBILITY

Paula Moraine

Jessica Kingsley *Publishers*
London and Philadelphia

First published in 2016
by Jessica Kingsley Publishers
73 Collier Street
London N1 9BE, UK
and
400 Market Street, Suite 400
Philadelphia, PA 19106, USA

www.jkp.com

Library of Congress Cataloging in Publication Data
Moraine, Paula.
  Autism and everyday executive function / Paula Moraine.
     pages cm
  Includes bibliographical references and index.
  ISBN 978-1-84905-725-7 (alk. paper)
  1. Autism spectrum disorders. 2. Cognition. I. Title.
  RC553.A88M667 2016
  616.85'882--dc23
                              2015025810

British Library Cataloguing in Publication Data
A CIP catalogue record for this book is available from the British Library

ISBN 978 1 84905 725 7
eISBN 978 1 78450 089 4

Printed and bound in Great Britain

This book is dedicated to the translators – to the parents, teachers, and friends who try valiantly to understand, interpret, and make sense of the autistic experiences in everyday life.

Contents

Preface

This book is born out of a unique and wonderful collaboration between a Finnish autistic savant and myself. Following the publication of my first book, *Helping Students Take Control of Everyday Executive Functions – The Attention Fix* (2012), translations were made into Dutch, Spanish, and Finnish. The Finnish translator, Pia Hämäläinen, contacted me, inquiring about accurately translating a specific term in the book from English into Finnish. This simple inquiry led to a sustained and lengthy email exchange on the topic of executive function in relation to autism because the Finnish translator herself is a highly educated, multi-lingual, autistic individual. Her questions were insightful, challenging, and relevant. An electronic friendship ensued, that extended a bit beyond the boundaries of the initial translation work. We began to trust each other with more and more of our individual concerns, and she shared personal experiences of autism that became formative in the writing of this book.

From the beginning of our communication, Pia would point out how students with autism could benefit from the approaches to everyday executive functions that she was translating from my book, indicating how she understood the role of executive functions for the autistic individual. Since her personal experiences were often expressed in fairly explicit theoretical and philosophical concepts, I found myself needing to translate her words into everyday English and into accessible language. Thus, the translated became the translator! Her thoughts were gloriously complex, and while they were clear to her, they were, at times, hard for me to understand. I had to concentrate to understand her, and found that as soon as I did understand, her thoughts were immensely valuable. It started to dawn on me that it did not matter if the thoughts of the autistic person were cloaked in very savant-like complex, theoretical frameworks, or if they were bound up in the autistic child's sensory experiences that could not be articulated; my job was to learn the "language" of the autistic person well enough to translate for them. So this book really became a book about translation – from one language to another, from one's personal experience to another, and about the translation between the autistic and non-autistic worlds.

Pia's personal description of her experience as an autistic adult is included in the Appendix at the end of this book. Her characterization of an adult's perspective on autism helps articulate how an autistic child's executive function can mature into an adult's executive function. Her story also highlights the struggle to first develop, and then integrate, executive skills into everyday life. Her intelligence, clarity, and honesty make her story accessible as well as instructive.

Introduction

Early in our email correspondence, Pia sent this rather provocative statement to me. At first I was taken by surprise that she placed teaching social skills on a slightly lower level of importance than is usual in relation to autism, but it soon became clear to me why she said this:

> I think that teaching executive function to people with autism is even more important than teaching social skills. Executive function needs to be learned first, and only then can we get to the social. I think that autism requires a higher degree of executive function organization to be functional than normalcy. The autistic mind is a space, often a chaotic one, that needs to be structured by the use of executive functions.

This statement places high importance on the need to understand the role of executive function in the individual with autism, but this is challenging because the term "executive function" is not that well known and understood; although it is gaining in popularity and is being used more frequently, it remains a relatively vague term for many. Most of us know maybe one person who has received a diagnosis of "executive dysfunction," while we might know several people diagnosed with "attention deficit hyperactivity disorder" (ADHD), which is automatically considered as executive dysfunction. Autism and ADHD can manifest in the same individual, but as distinct diagnoses. Executive function and ADHD are therefore strongly linked, so any discussion about executive function will naturally include a detailed discussion about attention.

Autism, on the other hand, is well known in modern times, and is defined, characterized, researched, and discussed in countless books, journals, articles, research papers, letters, and multi-media presentations. We are well into the 21st century, and nearly everyone knows someone with autism. It is not hidden, secret, or uncommon. Yet it remains a confusing, challenging, and often painful experience, not only for the individual with autism, but also for their families, friends, and loved ones.

Since there has already been so much written about autism, so many words spoken, do we really need any more? Maybe not, but if a new way of looking at the autistic experience helps even one person understand autism a bit better, it is worth adding one more voice to the conversation. This book offers a new, and in some cases novel, approach to autism and executive function, and a few guiding principles are addressed in this approach:

- the autistic mind can be seen as a chaotic space that needs order

- the autism experience can be structured via the use of executive functions

- the more functional the executive functions are, the more functional the social skills will become

- autism requires more executive function structure and more precise executive function structure than neurotypicality.

A common definition of the term "executive function" has to do with how we organize, plan, manage time, use our memory, and direct our attention. These are all discussed in detail throughout this book, and some differentiation is offered regarding the autistic and non-autistic experience of executive function. The more streamlined definition of executive function used in this book is that we use our executive functions to express how we *think*, what we *feel*, and what we *do* in relation to the world around us. These guiding principles can be approached through asking the questions, "What is the autistic experience of executive function? Does it differ from the non-autistic experience of executive function?" This is explained in more detail throughout the book more specifically as the question, "How does the autistic individual experience his or her thinking, feeling, or actions in a given situation?"

Asking the questions is easy; knowing how to "see" or "know" the answer is more difficult. An important idea for teachers, credited Parker Palmer (2007), is that we "teach who we are." As an educator, I find this to be very true as well as comforting. I can only be who I am; I cannot be someone else. The natural progression of this thought is that every student "learns who they are," in a highly individual way of receiving education and engaging in the learning process. Since so many of my daily contacts include parents, it is clear to me that parents also "parent who they are." Based on this fundamental approach to respecting the inviolate, personal, and individualized way of interacting with the world, the intention of this book is to honor the individual expression of autism without being too dependent on names and definitions of a "disorder." Every person diagnosed as being on the spectrum of autistic characteristics is still a unique, fabulously interesting individual.

Looking in on the experience of an autistic person from the outside, and being in the experience of the autistic person from the inside, are dramatically different, so it is no wonder that the non-autistic person understands so little about "autistic subjectivity." This is a term that I use in this book to identify what the subjective, personal, internal experience of autism is for the autistic individual. Naturally, this is hard for the non-autistic person to understand, but all efforts to be interested and to imagine what autistic subjectivity is for the autistic person will increase understanding and empathy. It is my hope that this book will transform any lack of understanding of autistic subjectivity, and that non-autistic readers as well as autistic readers of this book will find both clarity and comfort in its pages.

Preview of the book

This book is based on the principle of autistic subjectivity, which can be seen as the personalized manner in which the autistic individual experiences his or her world. These experiences are expressed in Chapter 1 through the metaphor of an autistic kaleidoscope, where the inner and outer experiences of the autistic individual may appear fragmented to the observer, but are clearly ordered and patterned experiences for the autistic person. For the autistic individual, the executive functions are what bring order and harmony to these varied, complex, and at times, fragmented, kaleidoscopic experiences.

Chapter 2 deals with the integration of experiences, beginning with the idea that all our experiences need to integrated and coordinated. The principle of salutogenesis as a way of balancing our experiences in a meaningful, manageable, and understandable way is discussed in detail. This links to the description of how an autistic person integrates and coordinates sensory input specifically. Coordinating and developing executive skills brings order into the chaos of the autistic experience, further supporting an individual's evolving sense of self.

This is a process that takes place over time, sometimes over a very long time. Along the way, we, as educators and parents, need to learn how to communicate with the autistic individual so we can become good listeners and good translators. We might need to learn new ways of communicating, since the autistic person might speak one of the "autistic languages" discussed in Chapter 3. These various languages are ways for the autistic individual to interact with the world, or to communicate in a way that makes the most sense to them. In many cases, the autistic language is the only way that autistic individuals can communicate, which emphasizes why it is so important for the non-autistic person to be flexible enough to learn about the autistic languages, and maybe even become proficient in the specific language of their autistic child.

Chapter 4 lays out tools, which I call Autistic Access Points, or AAPs, that can be used to establish effective executive skills.

Once a flow of communication is established through the use of the autistic languages, it is possible to work directly and explicitly on the executive functions through using one or more of the AAPs. These are often discovered through trial and error, or by simply observing the autistic individual carefully enough to perceive their preferred style of engagement and communication. They are both specific and generic in that a given child might need a very explicit, specific approach to one of the AAPs, such as relationships, yet having relationships is essentially a generic, human need.

After the AAPs are linked to the executive functions, Chapter 5 demonstrates how to identify a particular strength in the individual with autism, often one of the AAPs, and apply it to an emerging or developing executive function in support of that executive skill. I term this the "Executive Function Map," which serves the purpose of becoming a tool that resembles an Individual Education Plan (IEP), or an individualized plan of approach to the development of executive function or executive skills.

The precursor to understanding the role of executive function for the autistic person is the process of identifying the autism and getting the diagnosis. The next step often has to do with asking why normally expected developmental milestones for attention, social interaction, and academic progress are not being met. Once it is clear that autism is the primary factor, it then makes sense to consider how to support the development of executive function and the related developmental skills. This is discussed in detail in this book, but the following two stories from parents of autistic children describe the early experiences that led up to the initial diagnosis of autism, and the families' attempts at finding ways to both understand their child's experiences and then translate those experiences for others. They highlight not only the experiences of the family coming to grips with the fact of autism, but give insight into how simply engaging with the child, listening, observing, and believing them, leads to a level of insight. (Chapter 4 on

AAPs provides further details and ideas for understanding the experience of the autistic person.)

The first story re-tells one mother's long journey from the time before she received a clear diagnosis of autism, through her determined commitment to find a way to improve her child's life. She learns to translate her daughter's experience well enough to find the right help and interventions that include changes that needed to happen in her family and a complete change of schools. She set her daughter up to successfully acquire executive function skills through learning how to moderate her social interactions and establishing strong support for her attention (ADHD). These efforts directly support her emotional and academic experiences.

When my daughter was three years old, I started to get the unexpected reports from daycare about her continuing parallel play and not interacting with the other children. She was very close to me, but her odd behaviors became difficult for her grandparents, extended family members and our friends to understand and deal with. They all offered parenting and disciplinary strategies to me, as they, of course, assumed that her actions were due to bad parenting by a working mother. Kelly was often awkwardly outspoken and difficult to predict when we would go out to dinner, entertain, or visit other homes. We stopped getting invitations and had difficulty getting sitters. Whenever she encountered other children from school, we would cringe. There was always an awkward exchange, strange looks given to her by other kids, even giggling behind her back.

Kelly was always well behaved in school, but beginning in kindergarten, the teachers started to recommend that she attend summer school. This continued into the grade school years, and not understanding the education system, I would heed to their delays to address her struggles with her academic progress. Even though she was an excellent speller and very verbal, she had great difficulty with comprehension and math. At home she wrote her own songs and poems, but in school, she could not stay on point to answer questions correctly.

At Kelly's first grade teacher conference I expected to hear what a sweet and sensitive child she was. I was very surprised to hear that the teacher was concerned that Kelly was "on her way to being thought of as weird" by the other students because she liked to sing in the playground. The teacher was also very concerned about her organizational skills and inability to complete morning preparation in the classroom. She became increasingly anxious each morning, making sure she had everything in her backpack so that her first grade teacher would not be cross with her. In second grade we were blessed with an understanding and nurturing teacher that recognized that Kelly was a sensitive child who had great anxiety and peer issues. Her teacher recommended that we seek outside assistance. Kelly was diagnosed with severe ADHD.

Perceptions at school and by educators

In third grade, Kelly's social issues increased. She was made an example by the teacher for biting her nails and was made to put her hair up each day so that she could not play with it. The teacher sent her out of the room and told the other students to correct Kelly for these behaviors in the hope that she would be embarrassed into stopping. Of course they got worse. This particular teacher was the "favorite" of all students and parents. However, Kelly often mentioned that she knew that the teacher did not like her as much as the other students.

In fourth and fifth grades the school tried to provide her with a "fresh start" with new kids and with nurturing teachers, but it was too late. She was obsessed with disappointing her teachers and became paranoid that they were talking to each other behind her back. By the middle of fifth grade, I was receiving daily emails from the guidance counselor and special educator. Kelly changed from speaking up for herself with other kids and having an amazing sense of humor well beyond her years, to being a depressed child who fought going to school every day. She became a shell of herself. She was badly bullied by other girls, lost 11 pounds, was afraid to leave the house or be left alone, she could not be reasoned with or relieved during her episodes of severe panic. Kelly was placed on medication to give her some relief. It was recommended by the school that she begin the Home and Hospital school program[1] due to her frustrations and acting out at school. I took family and medical leave from my job, and with the help of her amazing advocate and tutor we found the help we needed in a counselor/social worker, psychologist and psychiatrist to finally end her suffering. Kelly missed most of her fifth grade year. It was not until this time that she was diagnosed with autism. I had to wonder what would have happened if I had found this out earlier. Would I have ended up with a less depressed, mentally ill child? I have no idea, but it was clear that I had work to do to help her through this point in her life.

Perceptions socially

We noticed early on that Kelly acted a bit different than her brother and other kids, but since we were unsure of what was going on, I would ask the pediatrician who assured me that Kelly was just exuberant. Not knowing what she would do or say at parties, at the grocery store, her brother's sporting events and at home gatherings made things very stressful for not just her father and I, but also her brother

---

1   The provision of instructional services to public school students who are unable to participate in their school of enrolment due to a physical or emotional condition. www.marylandpublicschools.org/msde/divisions/ studentschoolsvcs/student_services_alt/home_hospital/index.html

who was two years older. He was very embarrassed and chastised her for being "weird" at school and in front of his friends. Her brother had lots of friends and she noticed that she never had play dates or invitations to parties like he did. Her father started to discourage her from attending events. I ended up staying home with her on weekends while my husband and son attended my son's sporting events and parties. My son became resentful of the situation and all the time that I spent with my daughter. My husband not only rejected her need for his approval, but he refused to admit that she needed any additional outside help. He refused to attend her IEP meetings or accommodate transportation to her tutoring sessions when I worked full time. Finally, when she became so ill last year, I insisted that the entire family attend counseling. I learned the hard way that she was feeling the stress from the household even more that I was. I ultimately separated from my husband. With some initial financial support from my parents, I can now offer both kids a more calming and safe environment. A year later, Kelly is dong remarkably well. Her relationship with her father and my son has improved immensely, and so has my relationship with my son.

Recognizing AND acknowledging autism in our family

During our first parent meeting with our psychologist, he informed us that after evaluating Kelly, he truly felt that she was autistic. Further testing by her psychiatrist confirmed this diagnosis. The doctor could see my husband's anguish as he put his head in his hands. He asked the doctor if Kelly would be able to go to college, hold a job, or get married. The doctor eased my husband's mind by explaining how amazing Kelly really is, how smart and funny she is. He told us that things would get much easier socially as she gets older. He could also see the tension between my husband

and me. He told us that marriages can suffer greatly when there is a child with special needs. He recommended that we go home and watch the first season of "Parenthood" on Netflix. Later that night we sat down with her brother and started to watch. Starting in the very first episode, the story line dealt with a family finding out that their son's problems in school and with friends was due to autism. The show was OUR LIFE! The show even hit home with my son who could relate to the challenges of the sibling of the child. This was the awakening moment that our family had needed to find for five years. We could immediately both agree that she should attend a private school (no matter what we had to do to pay for it). It was not until this point that we could begin to heal AND provide the consistent support to Kelly that has changed her life and allowed her to become the happy, self-confident and brilliant young lady that she is growing into. My goal is for her to have the resources to be all that she can and wants to be, and I think that we are now finally on the right path.

Other families

In the past year I have talked to so many parents that have gone through the exact same experiences. Felt the pain seeing their child come home from school crying about being made fun of or bullied. I see them clench up at social gatherings and helicopter over every conversation and move that their child makes in public. I used to be the same way. Now I am just glad that she is better and happy and most of all, self-confident. I no longer even worry about what others think. My friends and family now understand and treat the entire situation differently. They have much more patience with comments that Kelly might make. And they refrain from giving any more parenting advice. If anyone does, I just politely walk away.

Kelly's story is not uncommon among families with autistic children. It shows how long the process was for Kelly's parents to get a diagnosis, deal with the family dynamics, and then finally find their way to a school situation that worked for Kelly. During these years, it is clear that they did not have time to focus on the executive skill development that Kelly was missing. They had far more pressing issues to deal with first.

The second story offers a wonderful example of how the mother of an 11-year-old autistic boy was able to discover what worked for her son by being sensitive, observant, and responsive. She was able to understand the factors that made a difference for her son, a process that is discussed in greater detail in Chapter 4 on AAPs. This mother understands the value of respecting her son's inner and outer relationships, his relationship with the elements of his environment, as well as his relationships with the people he meets. She found out what caused him distress, and what made him relax and able to interact with others. Once he felt safe and in a situation where his motivation and intentions were respected, he could use his executive skills and respond better in his school and family setting.

My son appreciates consistency; it is one of the most important things I can give him. He does not like others to over-react. He needs to finish his thought without interruption or he has to start over from the beginning. He needs to turn off/on the electronic devices or lights himself. If he turns it on or off, then it registers. If he doesn't turn it off, it doesn't register and he repeatedly questions whether it was done.

His lack of comprehension causes so much frustration for him and for us. Other people interject their advice regarding his situation and it only aggravates him. Our life seems so simple to fix looking in on it from the outside, but if the "fixers" were living in a similar situation, they would understand you couldn't fix it from the outside. Anyway, they don't need to find fault with my son; he finds enough fault with himself and he now knows that the odds are against him. If he were allowed to live his way, he would laugh and smile so much more. Others negatively influence this. He is not allowed to experience the world in the way he understands it. So many positive forward steps are denied to him simply because others do not understand him, and cannot incorporate his view of the world. They end up diminishing his accomplishments and successes. I understand this, though, because it is even hard for us to put together the pieces of what he likes and what he does not like.

For example, he doesn't like jigsaw puzzles, but when he was younger he loved a three-layer puzzle we had that consisted of the same picture of the house in different stages of development, one puzzle built upon the other. This is hard to understand if all you meet is his reaction to doing a jigsaw puzzle. You can easily miss that he has a much more complex level of understanding and feels comfortable in the multi-layer puzzle world. Most "outsiders" simply accuse him of being difficult and criticize me for not being a stricter parent.

His need for consistency shows up in school, too. When teachers talk, they change the words when they repeat something. He doesn't like this. When he reads, he can re-read because no words change, and this allows him to learn and remember. Reading silently to himself has no emotional intonation and is therefore easier for him. In school, he can't directly match Column A words to Column B definitions. However, if you separate them and shuffle them around, he can work it out until the words are matched correctly to the definition. Math that moves quickly from concept to concept is very hard for him. He does better with repetition and practice, and does not like to be asked to explain his work. He also has trouble with the many steps of some math word problems that are so many words and so little math.

He is great at remembering people who are kind, those who give him a chance to talk and do not overwhelm him. He is very polite when he is comfortable, and in those rare moments he grins and shows his dimples. He gets very upset when he sees bullying anywhere, even on TV or in a movie. He can tell the difference between when it is mean, and when it is a situation where everyone is simply having fun.

I try to use familiar words and familiar experiences to explain things he doesn't understand. He doesn't like interruptions when he is doing something. He also doesn't like to be told what to do, even in the form of advice. He can be told in advance, but don't interrupt what he is doing to tell him.

He appreciates consistency, and when his world is predictable and rhythmic, he relaxes, and the smile on his face says, "Thank you."

Again, this story is all too familiar. The mother shares the important insight that our autistic children suffer when we are unable or unwilling to adapt the environment to meet their needs, and instead demand that the autistic child adapt to our non-autistic environment. Both of these stories show us why it is so essential to have a flexible, insightful way of interacting with autistic children. We cannot read their behavior with the same set of translation tools we use with non-autistic children. It is also clear from these stories what a terrible impact our judgments and criticisms have on autistic children and their families. The remainder of this book offers ways of thinking and interacting with autism that could replace judgment and criticism with specific understanding and flexible thinking. The voices of these two sensitive mothers are inspiring because they helped alleviate their own child's suffering through careful observation and patient listening to what their child was trying to communicate.

1

The Autism Kaleidoscope

Key points

- Autistic subjectivity is the personal, internal experience of autism.

- The inner and outer experiences of the autistic individual may appear fragmented to the observer, but may be clearly ordered and patterned experiences for the individual.

- Order, organization, and executive skills are highly individualized. Each individual with autism will manifest a wide variety of strengths and weaknesses in relation to executive function.

- *Relating* to the non-autistic world rather than *adjusting* to it can be described as the autistic version of empathy.

- Autism is an experience of greater sensitivity and greater precision.

In this book, I discuss autistic subjectivity, or the personal autistic experience, from many perspectives. Since the inner and outer experiences of the autistic individual may appear fragmented to the observer, it can be difficult to remember that they may be clearly ordered and patterned experiences for the autistic person.

If we look through a kaleidoscope, the single image gets split into a fragmented, yet fully ordered, set of images. If we look through a single pane of glass, the image we see is simply the one image, unchanged. The autistic experience of the world can be more like looking through a kaleidoscope than a single pane of glass. The boy in the second example in the Introduction was one of the kaleidoscopic children. He was irritated by the single, one-dimensional puzzle, but was clearly engaged and fascinated by the three-layer puzzle. It was natural to him to see patterns and to make sense of them.

For most of us, when we look through a kaleidoscope, we see a single image that appears in multiple patterns and positions. We might look at each image and say, "Yes, that one is the true reflection of the original image!" Yet the image right next to it is also the true reflection of the original image, from a slightly different perspective, as are all the images that appear as a fractal reflection of the original image. Instead of making a pattern of the whole, we might all have a tendency to look at our own chosen image and its reflection, and feel comfortable that we have established a true relationship. The autistic perception of the world challenges that comfort. The autistic child may not have the necessary level of language or maturity to tell us exactly how their image is perceived, or they may not have the needed cognitive development to put their experience into words, but they are often much more able to deal with complex patterns than their non-autistic counterparts. Eventually, though, their perceptions and experiences need to be communicated, and how they manage to communicate these experiences is dependent on their development and use of different "languages" (discussed later, in Chapter 3).

The reader will hear the "voices of autism" throughout this book. The stories that are shared came about through many opportunities to hear directly from individuals with autism who could clearly articulate their personal experiences, and through parent, teacher, and therapist interviews. Whenever possible, the sources are the original words of the child, teenage, or adult individual with autism; it is clear that they are the best tellers of their own stories.

Autism has been referred to as a *pervasive developmental disorder*. While autism may, in fact, affect many areas of the individual's experience, and while it is also tracked through what are considered normal developmental milestones, the word "disorder" is unsettling. One of the important principles is that order, organization, and executive skills are highly individualized. Each individual, whether autistic or not, will manifest a wide variety of strengths and weaknesses in relation to executive function, so it becomes very difficult to be confident about naming what is "normal." Throughout the preparation of this book, myself and Pia contributed very different skills and insights. The autistic and non-autistic styles of perception make us both aware of very different areas of knowledge. What is normal for one person might not be normal for another, so what is normal for the non-autistic person may not be normal for the autistic person. Yet we find ways to adjust to one another and to understand each other.

Pia shared another challenging thought with me. She stated that the autistic person would prefer to *relate to* the non-autistic world, rather than *adjust to* the non-autistic world. She stated that relating to the non-autistic world rather than adjusting to it could be described as the autistic version of empathy. The autistic person might understand what is going on conceptually, understand the context and therefore understand what precipitates the behavior of the people involved, but will prefer to stop short of adjusting to those experiences. In this way, it is empathy through relating, and not empathy through adjusting, to the other's experiences or needs. As a mature adult, Pia was able to articulate this important thought. In the two stories in the Introduction at the beginning of this book we see how the parents of autistic children had to do the opposite – they were able to find access to empathy by adjusting to their autistic children rather than insisting on their child develop an ability to relate to them.

Throughout the book I discuss characteristics, share stories, and define what can be referred to as "autism-ness." "Autism-ness" is made up of the individual style of interacting with the world for the autistic person, or, to give it a more specific name, through "autistic subjectivity." Autistic objectivity and autistic subjectivity are described throughout the book. *Autistic objectivity* is what makes it possible for the autistic person to discern the features and principles of what they are interacting with, for example, "the cat." *Autistic subjectivity* is that essential part of self that approaches the interaction in an individualized or personal manner. For example, autistic subjectivity might make it possible for the autistic person to make a relationship with the "cat-ness" of the cat, but it takes longer to develop a relationship with the actual cat. Autistic objectivity, though, allows the autistic person to simply take the "cat-ness" at face value, making it possible to make a relationship based on that understanding.

These insights are offered as positive perspectives on autism. Since all knowledge is "perspectival," this book offers a kaleidoscope of perspectives and knowledge so the reader can draw his or her own conclusions. The reader is invited to see autism through different lenses and paradigms. Autism can be seen as a developmental disorder, as a neuro-psychiatric condition, or even as normal but with a difference of precision and sensitivity. This is a challenging thought, in that many of us have specific differences of precision and sensitivity as our response to the world around us. The autistic person, though, experiences the world with greater precision and heightened sensitivity. Examples of this can be observed in how the autistic person processes sensory information. What is simply a smell for one person could be an overwhelming and all-permeating experience for an autistic person. Other sensory experiences can come through with similar intensity – "normal" sounds can be distressing or even painful for the autistic person who experiences the world with greater sensitivity and precision. Textures can become an outrageous sensory assault, colors disturbing, and movement can become fascinating. In nearly every area of sensory input, greater sensitivity and greater precision intensify, magnify, and strengthen the impact of otherwise normal experiences for the autistic person. This can happen in the realm of thought too, and manifest as perseveration (getting stuck on one thought), or simply as intense analytical thought processes. Throughout this book, if the reader remembers that autism is an experience of greater sensitivity and greater precision, then all the autistic experiences described will make more sense. In whatever way the reader sees or understands autism, the following pages will hopefully expand horizons, stimulate insights, and inspire empathy.

2
Salutogenesis and Sensory Coordination

Key points

- Salutogenesis is based on the principle that there is a salutary, health-causing factor that arises out of integration or coherence, made up of these three experiences:

  - comprehensibility – we need to understand what is happening

  - meaningful – our experiences need to be relevant

  - manageable – providing the necessary tools to manage our experiences.

- Sensory *integration* allows us to integrate our sensory experiences, but for the autistic person, it is often a question of *coordinating* the sensory experiences, allowing the sensory input to be coordinated but not united.

- Sensory coordination allows the autistic person to focus on a single, chosen aspect of sensory experience, and not be overwhelmed with the whole sensory palate at once.

- Sensory coherence leads to a higher degree of access to the executive functions, and ultimately the autistic person becomes more socially functional.

A fundamental principle from my first book (Moraine 2012) is that of salutogenesis, originally discussed by Aaron Antonovsky (1987) from a medical perspective, which posits that there is a salutary, health-causing factor that arises out of a sense of "coherence." Coherence in this context means that our experiences fit together, they are related, and, most importantly, they give us a feeling of being integrated. Antonovsky attributes the three components of comprehensibility, meaningfulness, and manageability to the sense of coherence:

- *Comprehensibility:* how does the individual understand/ comprehend what is being asked of him/her? Does he/she understand what is going on in general? Does he/she have a sense of order or predictability in everyday experiences? Are the expectations of daily life clear?

- *Meaningfulness:* does he/she find the events and learning experiences of daily life interesting or meaningful? Does he/she care about the content being learned? Does he/she find the learning experience valuable, relevant, or meaningful?

- *Manageability:* does he/she have the necessary skills, ability, or support to meet the situation? Is the daily environment under control and manageable? Are the needed tools for managing the situation available?

These questions appear in every aspect of life, but how are these three components experienced specifically in the autistic universe? This is the fundamental question that defines "autistic subjectivity." The autistic person has a specific, defined, and individualized way of comprehending the world around him or her; he or she finds meaning in daily experiences based on personal interests, skills, and sensitivities, and manages daily life through what is possible, based on both developmental stages and natural gifts or talents.

Sensory integration meets sensory coordination

Sensory integration is a fundamental area of research, insight, and practice in the autistic community, the "gold standard" for understanding the use and integration of our senses. In order to process sensory input, messages coming in from the senses get sent through the nervous system and become a response. The feel of a fabric, the smell of food, the sound of a voice, these are all sensory inputs that produce a reaction. The reaction comes from how we process the sensory experience. One young autistic girl I worked with was particularly sensitive to smell, so as she came up to the lunch room, long before anyone else knew what was on the menu, she would start screaming, "No lasagna!! No lasagna!!" There was no stopping her until she was absolutely sure that she would not be forced to eat the lasagna. Touching her in this moment would be a mistake, and send her into an even deeper frenzy. The only thing that really helped was to simply offer her something else to eat so she could process the fact that she would not be confronted by lasagna. She was not a screamer under normal circumstances, and while her behavior did include repetitive behaviors, she was willing to work with me as her teacher and be guided through the daily activities. She was only nine, and she really wanted to learn, despite her very limited use of language. Her sensory "integration" was definitely affected, and in this case, the mere smell of the food she did not like sent her completely out of balance.

In a recent email conversation with Pia, I was inquiring in general about the impact of sensory experiences for the autistic person, and how to describe sensory integration from that perspective. The answer was surprising.

> It is my view that it is important to get sensory input through one's prevailing sensory channel/channels, and the rate of sensory input is crucial. Sensory input needs to be interpreted

and that is where mental structures, concepts, and conceptions play a crucial role. Hyper- and hyposensory experiences are also important. I personally believe in *sensory coordination* rather than *sensory integration*. By this I mean that one needs to coordinate, for example, vision and hearing, and not pay attention to the other senses. Sensory integration doesn't take into account the aspect-based, or single sensory experiences of autistic people. Sensory coordination is about taking the parts, or individual sensory experiences, and making them into a whole that can remain, unchallenged or unchanged by an outside person. Sensory integration is about the whole of the senses, and this may not respect the need to experience aspects of sensory experience individually.

This sudden and unexpected introduction to the concept of "sensory coordination" is exciting. Sensory coordination is a view that starts by identifying the fact that the individual has a preferred sensory input channel, such as visual, auditory, touch, etc. In the case of the girl who did not want to eat lasagna, it was important to wait for the reaction against the smell to calm down before introducing any other sensory stimulus such as touch or hearing. Talking to this child did not help right away, either, and looking back on that experience, I wonder if she was trying to coordinate her sensory experiences because she could not integrate them. Even calmly placing my hand on her shoulder and quietly encouraging her to stop screaming did not work, and I always sensed that I needed to communicate differently with her. If she was experiencing panic coming from being required to integrate too many sensory inputs at once, then no clever formulation of words from me would make a difference because what she needed was quiet – no talking, no auditory sensory input to process. She needed time to coordinate her sensory experiences, one or two at a time. This is how she managed her kaleidoscope – she made sense of the experiences she was able to understand, and created a pattern around them. Forcing her to expand this experience or reduce it would have simply caused her greater stress.

As described above, sensory input is interpreted individually, through the mental structures or "concepts." Another way to say this is that the concepts can be defined by how the individual relates to that particular sensory experience, or how the sensory experience is filtered. The filter does not always work perfectly, though. When there is not enough of a filter, the result is the hypersensory experience. "No lasagna!!" is an example of hypersensory experience. If the filter is too strong, not enough sensory information gets through, and results in the hyposensitive situation. Pain messages might not get through, so a person can be hurt, and if there were no physical, visible sign, no one would know to help. A stark example of hyposensitive processing is a young woman who fell when no one was looking. She did not tell anyone that she had fallen, and did not complain about any pain. I was working with her later that afternoon and noticed that her arm was actually at an odd angle. I asked if it hurt, but she told me it only hurt a little. I immediately took her to the doctor, and an X-ray revealed a complete fracture of the humerus, half-way between her elbow and her shoulder. How could such a massive amount of sensory input not come through as pain? Her pain receptors appeared to be completely blocked, and the physical, sensory channel of touch made little impression on this young woman. This stands in strong contrast to the child who could not even smell a specific food from a distance without a strong, overpowering reaction.

When parents describe situations with autistic children, the majority of descriptions follow the hypersensitive reaction, and the generally accepted response is to attempt to achieve sensory integration, or to integrate the sensory experiences. Sensory coordination means choosing the sensory channels, such as the visual and auditory channels, and temporarily shutting down access to the other channels of sensory input. Sensory coordination allows the autistic person to focus on a single, chosen aspect of sensory experience, and not be overwhelmed with the whole sensory palate at once. In an ideal world, the sensory experiences of the autistic person become coherent through sensory coordination. If this can happen, sensory coherence leads to a higher degree of access to the executive functions, and ultimately the autistic person becomes more socially functional.

Sensory experiences are often the key issue confronting families of autistic children. The following are reflections from Michael's mother describing Michael's difficulty balancing sensory experiences, and demonstrate how they impact the integration of his thoughts, feelings, and actions.

Michael needs to touch everything so he can gain information about the object or item. He wants to rub it on his face, rub his fingers over the object, and he can take in information about the item at the same time. If he isn't touching/feeling the item, his attention to any other information lessens. He seeks items out to use as part of his language experience when he talks with a peer or an adult. He prefers to insert the item into the conversation by showing it during his explanation or request. Without physical input, he often doesn't conceptualize the item's components or parts. He learns much faster and with sustained accuracy when the item is present and he has access to physical input. He will also appear to be trying to rub off the touch because he will repeatedly rub his skin after being touched.

From around the age of three to six, Michael would often remove any or all articles of clothing at inappropriate times. His need to adjust his clothing completely overrides anything that is happening around him at any time. It is becoming increasingly uncomfortable for others in social settings, especially when he simply disrobes.

Over time he would scream, hit, and occasionally bite us to avoid or delay having his toenails cut. There were several behavior modification plans in place, such as Applied Behavior Analysis (ABA). Breaking down his behavior into smaller increments, and giving him specific feedback and rewards for successfully mastering that increment of behavior, helped us to help him scaffold skill after skill needed to tolerate this process. Another way to say this is that we helped him coordinate his behaviors rather than integrate them and conquer them all at once.

He consistently avoids certain food textures and began limiting his food choices at two years old. He repetitively only accepts crunchy foods in an attempt to receive the desired input. We work with an occupational therapist (OT) because he needs to be taught how to accept, manipulate, and swallow foods that present an unexpected feeling in his mouth, such as peas, peaches, peanut butter, etc. We have worked continuously for five years using a target-based eating plan, and he now has more than 20 foods in his repertoire.

When Michael brushes his teeth and hair he self-imposes rules, following certain steps and using certain amounts of acceptable pressure or acceptable tools to complete the task. We use electric toothbrushes, as well as gentle sensory stimulating dental tools which have helped desensitize his hypersensitive mouth over time.

He uses touch for communication of thoughts or feelings instead of finding appropriate words or functional language. He flicks his brother's hair to convey disappointment, frustration, or disapproval, and rubs or plays with his brother's hair to share affection, agreement, or to get attention. He rubs my hair or his teacher's hair to find solace or security. His clothes can't have any tags or seams that are bumpy, and the waists of his clothing need to have the correct amount of pressure. He would rather wear clothes two or more sizes too small to achieve the preferred compression tension. He wants fabric to cover his arms at all times regardless of temperature. He throws himself into furniture, floors, etc. as a way of seeking feedback.

Michael doesn't say he is tired or hungry. Instead, he demonstrates behaviors and his ability to navigate environments plummets quickly. For a long time he didn't express pain or distress but communicated with screams, self-injurious behaviors, tantrums, eloping (running off), etc.

Repetitive movements are ever-changing as he develops and matures. Replacement behaviors are being taught all the time, and some repetitive movements have been extinguished through behavior modification. This is good news, except that as one behavior diminishes, a new one appears. He finds a video game reinforcing and will create the video game movements with his body or repeat the video game noises over and over in order to access the reinforcing activity, even when the video game is turned off.

He will always find a wall to walk next to and slide his fingers, hands, or whole arm along the structure to get whatever input feels best. At times, he appears to be dragging his body against structures and it can be dangerous.

Most car trips were spent trying to distract Michael from staring out his window. He looks so odd watching things go by because his head whips or rolls back and forth from side to side for the entire trip. We discovered that his eyes focused on objects only a few feet in front of the car and as soon as the object passed he would repeat. He never saw the big yellow school bus or the cow in a meadow I was desperately trying to point out, because he was hyper-focused on items passing by only feet away from his window.

He has great difficulty planning and executing a motor task. He struggles to plan repetitive everyday movements such as walking down stairs. He has to be explicitly taught to get on and off a bike; otherwise his only strategy is to deliberately fall off, over and over. Pushing pedals in opposite movements requires attention that seems impossible while he is moving through space. He never rode a tricycle.

Odors that are detectable by us can cause him to vomit. He avoids people, places, and activities when he feels bombarded by many common smells. Riding in a car with leather seats would produce tantrums, but he didn't have the language skills for a long time, so he couldn't communicate what was bothering him. He didn't pick up on the social cues of others, so holding his nose was not meaningful to him, and we remained confused about the leather seats for a long time. Cooking smells, restaurant smells, exhaust, and food odors can cause him to elope. He smells his food before placing it in his mouth. His intense need to smell the food, and the need for routine, combine to intensify the behaviors and can make him more rigid.

He turns lights off if he is allowed. He prefers dark to light, and wears sunglasses year round, even on cloudy days when I would guess they aren't necessary; Michael squints in the regular light, and appears to be in pain.

He withdraws when he cannot physically connect with a person of interest. For him to share an idea or an experience, he needs to be connected to the adult through a pairing process that is intentional and ongoing. He uses physical touch to meet the need of security and safety.

Michael creates his own sounds to reproduce a certain part of an experience that was reinforcing and when the specific preferred activity is no longer available, Michael will reproduce the sounds over and over to re-create that good feeling. He repeats video sounds, scripts lines from movies or commercials, etc. Michael cannot focus on one sound if there are competing sounds. He often will notice the low hum or beeping of the microwave so intensely that he cannot respond to a question unless the sound is identified and stopped.

He was taught to communicate with words by explicitly teaching each target word through the different verbal operants in order to construct meaning. He needed to repeat the word and touch the item to construct a mental image that could be transferred from setting to setting. He could ask for a cookie when in our kitchen, but if he saw a picture of a cookie, or if someone offered him a cookie in a different setting, Michael could not understand or produce the word.

Michael doesn't understand that his perspective is not the same as the perspective of others around him. He assumes that I see what he sees, even if I am not with him. He would refuse to answer or have a tantrum when I asked about an event because he thought I already knew. He becomes very frustrated when I do not know what he is trying to relate to me about an experience because he assumes I have the entire sequence rolling in my mind's eye, just as he does. He doesn't speak in complete sentences when he wants to connect with others about a topic on his mind. He just starts his "download" of thoughts without noticing if the other person is paying attention to what he is saying or not.

Michael is learning through specific instruction that other people have thoughts that are different than his own. He is learning how to notice nuance and subtle changes in others' behaviors to indicate intention, feelings, and expectations. Without specific intervention, he is not able to intuitively identify the "hidden curriculum" and repair miscues as he navigates the world. He always assumes that the way he perceives the situation is the truth for everyone involved. When he tries to be funny to get a peer's attention, Michael cannot figure out why the friend is not laughing if the joke isn't appropriate or funny. He will simply start interjecting another joke over and over. Meanwhile, the joke might be part of the script from a movie he thought was funny. He will just start telling the joke and can't read a person's face to understand that he is hurting someone else, or that they simply don't know what he is talking about.

Parents reading this description will likely relate to at least parts of Michael's story. These parents had to "scaffold skill after skill" just to make it possible to cut Michael's nails. They were working on sensory coordination rather than sensory integration because they were narrowing the sensory demand down to fewer channels at once, so Michael could learn how to be touched enough to allow his nails to be handled. They identified the sensory overload caused by the texture of food, separating the textures so he could learn to tolerate them one at a time. They worked hard to build on Michael's sensory coordination one small bit at a time. They accepted that it is difficult to read situations with enough precision to understand what the child is really saying with their screaming and sensitivity to touch. Parents, like Michael's mother, find themselves in the position of translating the child's behavior and trying to speak the language of their child's sensory experience. Gradually, over time, it changes, and in Michael's case, the more actual language he gained, the more he could express and explain his experiences. The more the parents coordinated his sensory demands, the more Michael was able to accept the sensory experiences and incorporate them into his daily experiences.

3

Autistic Languages and Communication

Key points

- Non-autistic individuals use emotional, social/ pragmatic, visual, conceptual, kinesthetic, and sensory language every day.

- The autistic individual may access only aspects or components of each language, resulting in what is essentially a new language.

- What might appear as a random gesture might, in fact, be targeted and intentional communication from the autistic child to us.

- This requires some refined translation skills on the part of the teachers and parents.

Language and communication are the most precious, fascinating, and complex modes of engagement we have as human beings. We take communication for granted most of the time; when we speak, we assume others understand what we said, and we assume others grasp our meaning. Yet, despite our best efforts, what we say is often not heard, and what we mean is often misunderstood. Since language and communication is so important, pervasive, and complicated, how much more challenging does it become for an autistic person who might process language fundamentally differently? Exactly what language are we speaking with another person? If they speak English, Spanish, French, Chinese, etc., we expect to work hard at the communication and do not assume that we will understand everything correctly, unless we put some real effort into the process of learning about the other person's language. Our language is our subjective way of filtering information from the world around us, and our language becomes a tool on our subjective path of learning.

Educators and psychologists understand the learning process based on models of learning theory, attempting to define the nature of learning and the learning process. Psychologists might consider behavioral, biological, cognitive, psychodynamic, or social modes of learning. Educators will consider learning based on the cognitive, affective, or motor skills used in learning. Regardless of the learning theory used, the nature of learning is dependent on, and affected by, the individual learning style, which becomes the "language" of choice for most communication. Even though people spend most of their lives as adults, childhood experiences and communication styles set the tone for the individual's lifespan. The presence of autism, which influences the entire development of communication and language skills, is a central factor influencing life-long communication skills.

We can talk about "autistic languages" if we establish some understanding of the similarities and differences of autistic and non-autistic communication. The non-autistic version of the following "languages" help shed light on just how differently the autistic individual processes the same components of communication. These languages, or ways of communicating, are used every day in non-autistic communication, though the autistic individual may access only aspects or components of each language, resulting in what is essentially a new language that requires translation.

Emotional language

Emotional language focuses on how we feel – happy, sad, frustrated, enthusiastic, etc. It allows us to express how our actions make us feel – "playing soccer makes me happy," "folding my clothes is difficult." Emotional language also makes it possible to focus on how someone else feels, and then we can feel empathy for that person.

Emotions are to human experience what tones are to music. Music consists of tones that arise in the interval between two notes. What lies between note "c" and note "e" is an interval with qualities and characteristics that do not belong to the "c" or "e," but only arise between the two. Emotions are also born in interaction. It is this interaction that gives rise to the emotion. The interaction can be between people, thoughts, or events, but it colors and forms the emotional response. The similarities between music and emotions stop here, though, because what happens between "c" and "e" in music is always the same, repeatable interval of tone. In emotional responses, there is no repeating pattern. Each emotional response is different in some way to any other emotional response. This is partly what causes so much distress to the autistic person who seeks sameness and repetition. Not only does each interaction change a bit, but also the response to each interaction is different.

We have generally accepted genres of emotion that we try to agree on such as happiness, sadness, anger, joy, frustration, irritation, and so on. Just as there are an infinite number of colors, so there are an infinite number of emotional experiences. Even within the same individual, the emotional variety is staggering.

Sympathy is a common expression of emotion, and we value the expression of sympathy in others. The definition of sympathy is having a fellow feeling or "feeling with" the other that manifests as interest, concern, sorrow, and pity. The opposite of sympathy is antipathy, generally accepted to be a negative or hostile feeling of aversion or dislike.

Empathy brings us into the experience of the other, and can be described as feeling with the other through compassion that is based on either having been in that situation, having experienced such a situation, or having the ability to fully picture what the other is going through. The term was first used in the art world as the ability to infuse the art with one's personality. Now it is used as a generic word indicating a level of merging with the other's experience. The problem with empathy is that we need to have some way of measuring the other's experience. If someone says, "I am sad," then an entire array of measurements launch as a way of understanding what level of sad is meant. Is the person sad because there is no dessert at dinner, sad because the dog died, sad because someone said something hurtful, etc.? Sad might elicit only sympathy – "I am sorry you don't get dessert tonight" – or empathy – "I know how terrible it is to have your dog die. Mine died last year and it was awful." The closer the response gets to empathy, the more involved the individual is with the emotions of the other. Referring to the mental images that are used in visual language (see "Visual language" below) it is important to note that empathy is not possible without the ability to form mental images and create a picture of what the other might be going through.

Emotions are subjective by nature. We try to bring a measure of objectivity into them with a happy face to indicate happy, and a "yuck" face to indicate something harmful or distasteful. These generic expressions are important, but are not automatically transferrable symbols. Many autistic people can see these images and not understand that they are meant as universal symbols of a universally understood feeling of happy, sad, or "yuck." It is the very nature of the universality of these symbols that is difficult for some autistic children. Adjusting or adapting the happy face to so many different nuances of happy can take time to learn.

In academic settings, a lack of empathy can impede reading comprehension. Since reading comprehension is dependent on forming mental images and having previous experiences to work with, the autistic reader will come to very different conclusions about the reading, and therefore have a very different comprehension of the text. If the book is written in emotional language, and the autistic reader reads using pragmatic language (see "Social and/or pragmatic language" below), then without any preparation or pre-reading skills, the autistic reader will have very little comprehension.

One way to prepare the autistic reader for comprehension is to establish a knowledge base about the text prior to reading through creating mental pictures that the reader can call on while reading. Who is in this text? What are their names? What do they look like? What is the story about? Where is it happening? What is the time period? What is the setting? It is common practice to ask these questions after the text is read, because we assume the reader is gradually building a picture while reading. We also assume that the reader will remember the content of the text, particularly the emotional elements, well enough to build pictures of events and characters as they evolve through the story. Autistic students can benefit greatly from pre-reading and preparing the pictures from the text as a way of building an emotional scaffold for comprehension.

Social and/or pragmatic language

Social and/or pragmatic language is the foundation of our interactions with others. We speak with words, gesture, and even thoughts. From our early days of infancy, we begin learning social language through exchanging gazes, reaching out to touch the world, and experiencing the warmth and care from others. Throughout child development, social language is mixed into every day and every interaction we have, so we are learning social language simultaneously with many other languages.

Social and/or pragmatic language allows us to adjust the way we speak in different situations.

> **Pragmatic language skills make it possible for children to greet an adult cheerfully, politely, or formally, and then speak the language of a friend when playing with peers in a social setting or on the playground.**

Social skills are based on the capacity to interact with others, understand effective distance from the other, and the ability to participate in reciprocity and turn-taking. Teaching social skills or social communication is one of the first items on an educational plan for an autistic student. The quote from Pia at the beginning of this book states that it is more important to teach executive function first, and then social skills. This is more than just a matter of word choice and semantics; in my experience, executive skills are closely linked to the social skills we need for social language, and are needed as a foundation for building social skills. A conversation based on social language contains identifiable components:

- interaction – the action between the speakers, rather than action/reaction

- distance – sensitivity to personal space and how close or far away the other person needs to be

- reciprocity – the give and take on the same theme, as equal partners in the conversation

- turn-taking – no one in the conversation takes too much or too little of a turn, but knows when to initiate and inhibit their contribution.

Social language includes sympathy, antipathy, and empathy. *Sympathy* gives the conversation some needed engagement and even passion for the other or for the theme. *Antipathy* indicates engagement too, even if the engagement is based on determining that it is distasteful or disagreeable. *Empathy* is the highest level of social language because it requires background knowledge and experiences, mental imaging, or the ability to imagine what the other is experiencing, and context, which brings objectivity into the interaction. Developmentally, the younger the child, the more the child engages with only sympathy and antipathy, and only later acquires empathy.

Social language is developmentally based and learned in stages. The pre-school child engages in a world of imitation and play. They can enter a world of imagination, full of characters and events that are real to them, even if no one else sees or hears this world. They often exist in parallel to other children, playing happily along in their world while the child next to them plays happily in his or her own world of imagination. If this world of play is disrupted, the child can be very distressed, but will usually adjust to being back in the same world as everyone else. The autistic child can also enter a world of his or her own, and happily exist in parallel to other children, but might need a longer time to mature into the social level of reciprocity and playing with others. Parallel play and personal experiences are still valid and valuable steps along the way of learning social play. The social stages of play and social interaction are essential for the development of social language, and these must be explicitly taught to the autistic child who is naturally stuck at the stage of personal experience and parallel play. Teaching a child to move beyond this phase can be done, but it is most effective if it can start at the level of the child's experience. As a teacher of young children, I quickly learned one way to deal with social conflict, when neither child had the necessary maturity and social skills or language.

Tim and Ellen are eight years old. They are playing hard on the playground, but things quickly get difficult between them. Soon, Ellen is crying, running to me saying that Tim hit her with a stick. Tim is close behind, hollering that he didn't hurt her – she was the one who did it and wouldn't share the swing.

Me: "So, Tim you can sit here on my left, and Ellen, you can sit here on my right."

They both sit down, still trying to talk, so I quietly tell them I am going to ask each one to tell me what they did, and just what they did, without a word about what the other one did.

Me: "Ellen, you can start. What did you do?"

Ellen: "Tim hit me!"

Me: "Not what Tim did, just what you did."

Ellen: "I was swinging on the swing. Tim kept yelling that he wanted it."

Me: "Not what Tim did, just what you did."

Ellen: "I told him no, I was swinging."

Me: "Then what?"

Ellen: "Then Tim started yelling at me."

Me: "Not what Tim did, just what you did."

Ellen: "Well, I kicked and hit at him a few times, and I got him once."

Me: "Where did you get him?"

Ellen: "On his shoulder."

Me: "Anything else that you did?"

Ellen: "Well, I called him stupid."

Me: "Anything else?"

Ellen: "No."

Me: "Tim, what did you do?"

Tim: "She wouldn't let me have the swing!"

Me: "Not what Ellen did, just what you did."

Tim: "I asked her for a turn."

Me: "What did you say?"

Tim: "I yelled she had been on the swing too long."

Me: "And then?"

Tim: "I called her stupid back."

Me: "Then?"

Tim: "I hit her with a stick."

Me: "Ellen, do you have anything you want to add?"

Ellen: "No."

Me: "Tim, anything to add?"

After a slight pause...

Tim: "Can I tell her I am sorry?"

Me: "Yes, you can say it to her directly if you want."

Tim leans around me and says he is sorry to Ellen, Ellen says she is sorry, too. I wait a moment, then ask if both are ready to go play again and they run off together and play without further incident.

This interaction is important because it illustrates how children can be taught to recognize their personal actions, and listen to the other describe the situation from the other's perspective. Although autistic children find this very difficult at first, once they know what is happening, they also benefit from this explicit model of reflection and interactions. This encourages collaboration and conflict resolution without ever engaging in blame. Blame assumes that the blamer can judge the actions of the other, and in this situation I wanted to teach social conscience through social language. I was not interested in blame, since the natural result of a blame/shame scenario is punishment or humiliation.

This approach employs many of the tools that can be effectively used to teach social skills: taking turns/speaking one at a time; affirming what is said; speaking softly; asking for clarification; and summarizing. This approach also teaches executive function skills directly because each child was given a safe and protected situation in which they could call to mind their own actions, reflect on them without fear, and make a new decision about future actions. There was no fear of anger, punishment, or repercussions. All their energy went toward calling up mental pictures of their own actions, reflecting on those actions, and making new decisions for the future. These are the most basic actions of using executive functions as social skills. Learning about being social, or learning to speak in social language, is done best when the fear, anger, shame, and blame is removed from the equation completely. Teaching social language teaches collaboration and teamwork without conflict; social controls that include give and take; and conflict resolution so they can handle disagreements calmly and without aggression.

Social and/or pragmatic language is a communication style that relates to the explicit, realistic meaning of the words, as well as social meanings. A wonderful, humorous, example of this style of language can be found in the Amelia Bedelia children's stories.[1] In these stories, Amelia is a friendly woman who is employed as a maid. She is asked to "dust the living room," so she fetches the talcum powder from the bathroom and sprinkles it all over the room, giving every piece of furniture a "good dusting." She quite literally does what she is asked to do. Another example is the Dr. Sheldon Cooper character that portrays an adult version of speaking pragmatic language in the TV series, *The Big*

---

1   Parish, P. (2005) *Amelia Bedelia Helps Out*. New York, NY: Greenwillow Books.

Bang Theory.[2] Sheldon's character is hilariously pragmatic, much to the entertainment and dismay of all the other characters on the show. This show is presented as a comedy, but it has a serious, underlying message. A person who sees the world pragmatically cannot be simply told they are seeing it all wrong. They cannot be forced to give up their natural way of processing language. Pragmatic language makes sense to them. It is fitting that this character is a scientist, since science, as a field of study, does have room for pragmatic thinking.

Pragmatic or social language gets more complicated when applied to human relationships, though. The realm of interpersonal relationships, intention, innuendo, gesture, and body language are foreign forms of communication to those who speak autistic pragmatic language. A gesture that indicates, "Please help me pick these things up off the playroom floor" at home cannot be used at a friend's house since it is not the same playroom floor as the one at home. Autistic pragmatic/social language needs to be re-constructed explicitly for each situation, since the essence of the gesture or the meaning of the words changes as soon as the environment changes.

Pragmatic language is also the language of practical actions. It makes sense to do things in a certain order, in a certain way, and being asked to change this order can be disturbing. It is frequently connected to routine. Marla, a young autistic adult, brought pragmatic language together with her daily routine in a fascinating way. Whenever she was doing one activity, such as folding her laundry, she would have a running dialog that always revolved around the same topics. When she was engaged in a different activity, such as washing dishes, her conversation topics would change, and even the tone and tenor of her voice changed. Visitors to the house would always find her engaging and pleasant, and even be surprised that she was not living on her own. If they came more frequently to visit, they would see that

---

2   A CBS Television show created by Chuck Lorre and Bill Prady.

her language did not change, and her repetitive, pragmatic way of speaking about things was actually more of a pattern that she was stuck with and could not change.

Pragmatic language is the language of consistency, facts, and action. It is not the language of creativity and nuance. It is also the vehicle for social language which allows us to manage the socially acceptable language used for greeting people, politely asking for something, etc. Marla sounded very social on first meeting, but on the second or third visit it was clear she was not engaging in the give and take of social discourse. If asked directly, she would answer questions based on the obvious (to her). One of the social areas we worked on attempted to help her answer the questions, "How are you?" or "How do you feel?" Her first answer would be to start speaking about a sore shoulder or a cut on her finger. She did not understand that the question was a generic, socially polite type of question that did not require an answer other than, "I am fine, how are you?" These conversations were hardest for her, since they were not connected to her work or activity, and they were not meaningful to what she was doing at that moment. Eventually, we managed to make these responses fit her repetitive patterns, so even though she never felt comfortable with these open-ended, socially polite exchanges, she learned what pattern of responses were acceptable, and was able to use them as needed.

Visual language

Looking at pictures helps us understand the meaning and content of the scene we are seeing. Visual language helps us form mental images, which in turns improves our comprehension of the situation. Visual language brings us together with others, so that when someone is talking about soccer, we can form the mental image of playing soccer, and participate in the conversation through visual language.

Michael's mother shared another important story with me, describing how Michael pictures what he sees.

I find myself glancing up at the clock, getting a bit nervous that it is time to leave. Michael doesn't read my signals, doesn't follow my gaze up to the clock to see that it is time to go. He is looking just past my head, at the kitchen cupboard. Now he is confused, because there is no clock on the kitchen cupboard, so he can't figure out why I keep talking about time. Why do I keep motioning to something that is behind his head? Agitation begins to set in, and I think it is because he lacks a sense of time. So I say with my careful words, "Michael, we only have three minutes before we need to be ready to go." He understands my words, but cannot connect them to the clock and asks why I keep talking about the clock. Then it dawns on me! This has nothing to do with his sense of time – it has everything to do with the fact that he cannot picture what I see. He thinks that what he sees is what I see. My vision and his vision are not separate in his mind. If he sees it, then I must be seeing it. There is no clock on the kitchen cupboard, so there is no reason to be talking about looking at the clock.

"Michael, what are my eyes looking at?" This is a seriously difficult question for him. I have to put my head next to his, getting our vision lined up together, and ask it again. Then I turn my head a bit, and ask him again. "What are my eyes looking at?" As I circle around to face him, when I ask again, he can follow that now I am looking at him, and he is looking at me. It is another step for him to realize when I look up I am looking at what is above or behind him, since that requires him to recognize the space behind him. This is a slow process for Michael, and we repeat it as often as needed, since every change of environment is a fully new situation, and he doesn't understand the idea of generic space. The space

behind him is very specific to the precise environment we are in at that moment.

Visual language has everything to do with what is actually seen. It is very concrete – "I see it in front of me so I accept that it exists." It gets confusing when the autistic person does not grasp that others see something different than what he or she sees. Autistic vision has just that one, personal perspective. This poses a challenge for the non-autistic person to stop and imagine the differences between the two visual fields. It is a good exercise to imagine a situation from a new perspective, which provides an opportunity to think about things differently. There are many ways to experience this. For example, when riding in a train, first sit facing the way the train is moving, then switch and sit facing opposite of the way the train is moving. Some people have no difficulty with this, but others cannot stand to sit "the wrong way around." Another example from the classroom happened when I was trying to convey a new lesson, and I wanted to see if the students had understood, so I asked for a volunteer to become "teacher" and I would be the "student." One student did volunteer, and as that student went up to the front, instead of standing at the back, I sat down in her desk. I looked around, a bit startled, since I had no idea that this was the perspective for that student every day. How did the board look to her? What could she see? What was difficult to see? I saw the room through her eyes, rather than through mine, and it was indeed "eye-opening"! Since that day, I have been far more sensitive to imagining the world through the eyes of someone else, but this is difficult for children like Michael. He has to be taught how to "see what I see," since his default position is to assume that everyone else sees only what he sees.

There is another level to visual language, and that is the mental image, or mental picture. It can be difficult for an autistic person to identify and describe the image in their mind. This often manifests in reading comprehension. If I ask my students what they picture when they read a story or a passage in a textbook, the conversation ends up something like this:

"Jeffery, what is this passage about?"

"It's about two boys."

"Yes, and what are the boys doing?"

"They probably want to play their video games."

"Does the passage say anything about video games?" (I ask this because the story is set in the 1800s, well before video games were available.)

"I am sure that is what they are talking about."

In this example, Jeffery does not form a mental image based on the content of the story. His visual language is pre-set, so he sees the pre-set images and pictures in his mind. Jeffery's intelligence is not in question, so if he actually had a pre-set image to refer to in his mind, he could access that picture and easily comprehend the content of the story.

Students with autism need explicit preparation for reading comprehension. If they are not immediately flexible enough to form mental images related directly to what they read, then preparing the mental images in advance of the reading is essential. Here is how the conversation goes when I have the opportunity to prepare a student for reading.

"Jeffery, this story is about two eleven-year-old boys. That is the same age as you and your friend Sam. They lived in the 1800s. What do you know about the 1800s? Since they lived in the Midwest, what do you picture as the landscape around them? What kind of school did they attend? How did they get home from school? What do you imagine they did after school?"

Such questions might be accompanied by some visual images quickly found in a book or on the internet as we talked, and I would add other sensory information to the picture so his visualization could include sights, smells, tastes, textures, temperatures, etc. Both autistic and non-autistic students benefit from this kind of imaging, but autistic students need this very targeted preparation in order to establish some pre-set images they can later recall during reading. They need practice creating mental images that relate to the world around them, so they do not get stuck in their personal pre-set world of pictures.

Conceptual language

Conceptual language makes it possible to explain things using words and concepts rather than pictures. A conceptual thinker might give a verbal description detailing the events of the day, or re-telling all the steps of how something was made. Conceptual thinkers can also present, or write, the pro and con arguments of an issue with ease.

Conceptual language is a way of understanding language through scientific and/or philosophical meaning, or by just simply using concepts to communicate. Conceptual thinking is associated with adult thinking. We do not expect the young child to learn through concepts, but rather through experiences. This is one of the biggest challenges in modern education, because the current Western education system is geared toward teaching concepts that rarely have an experiential component. The concepts are taught in a form that is testable or assessable. This is equivalent to teaching the brain but not the heart or hands. In my experience, most children learn naturally through hands-on, practical activity. Children also learn through imaginative pictures and stories. Concepts generally join the party much later and become a direct vehicle for learning in the pre-teen and early teen years. Some autistic children speak conceptual language at a very young age, and are quite at home in an educational system that teaches concepts – wonderfully predictable, repeatable concepts! These children appear a bit like miniature adults.

I worked with one student who was only able to use conceptual language to communicate. His specialty was animals – all of his communication was based on animal facts and knowledge. Reading came naturally to him, so specific reading instruction was not needed.

During the year I worked with Liam, he was not able to compose any written work that was not about animals. He resisted doing any math unless we could find a way to base it on animal facts and information. Socially, Liam had to be taught how to spend time with people and not hijack the conversation to talk about animals. At that time, he was given the label of high functioning Asperger's syndrome. Liam did not respond well to emotional language. It did not help to show frustration or impatience to him. He would become agitated and drown out the emotions he felt coming toward him by re-establishing his animal theme. He could calm down if no one interrupted him as he retreated into his conceptual, predictable world. Liam was not pragmatic in relation to other people, but he was a bit pragmatic in relation to his animals. He took the scientific knowledge he acquired at face value. He particularly liked books that were written in a factual, encyclopedic tone. He certainly did not like to read anything that was open for interpretation, or that was expressed in a metaphor. Concepts were not metaphors for him; concepts were facts, and once learned, needed to remain unchallenged.

Liam is a good example of a young teenager fully engaged in conceptual language, yet missing the earlier components of learning. Earlier stages of learning included the sensorimotor experience, which Liam avoided as much as possible. He limited sensory input whenever possible, and by establishing himself with his animals, he could reject any sensory engagement that was not on his "animals" terms. He also did not engage in the early pre-conceptual stage of learning through doing, exploring, and asking millions of questions. Everything was already pre-set, pre-determined, and pre-ordered. He was not flexible enough to learn anything that was not already written in his animal books. Liam went straight for the concrete stage of learning and stayed there. He did not move on toward the stage of abstract thinking, either. It seemed like he parachuted into the concrete thinking phase, and simply stayed there, fully able to ward off anything as pesky as emotional engagement or emotional language. Concrete language saved Liam from the world of unknown expectations and emotional innuendo. Eventually, through the process of maturing, he was able to gain greater access to emotional language by using the strength of his conceptual language. He was able to understand the concept of emotional interaction, and that led him to the insight he needed to be able to use and understand emotional language. In this case, the strength of one language opened up the door to another language.

Conceptual language can also be used as a framework for social situations. For example, what is the organizing principle, value system, or concept that is playing a key role in a conversation? One person might be participating in the conversation thinking of him or herself as guiding the conversation in a specific way, while another might be simply looking for social contact. Conceptual language also gives us common ground, and allows everyone to address the same theme or content in a conversation. This prevents one person from speaking about how to build a tree house while the other person begins talking about an interesting boat they saw while on vacation. Conceptual language also allows us to understand common values, even if they have different manifestations. We start teaching about these common values by way of imitation with the young child, and gradually add the conceptual language as the child matures. The autistic child does not always learn easily through imitation, so as the autistic child matures we need to take the imitative to start this conceptual conversation. If we can accept that their experiences are real and valid, we can allow their experiences to become a wonderful starting point for communication, and find common ground together.

Kinesthetic language

Kinesthetic language is the language of movement and touch. We use kinesthetic language when we move, dance, play a musical instrument, play sports, make crafts, bake bread, model/sculpt, knit, etc. We use it in combination with many other senses, but movement is involved nearly every time.

Kinesthetic language speaks through every sensory channel, but can be referred to as the sensory language of movement overall. A highly "sensitized" individual might be fluent in kinesthetic language, yet not be able to master processing his or her sensory experiences. Sensory integration is another way to describe how the senses are processed. The term "sensory coordination" was introduced in Chapter 2, and this term can guide us in our discussion of kinesthetic language. The term "kinesthetic" usually refers to sensory input that is physical, tactile, or movement-based. If we learn best by touching or doing, we are generally referred to as a kinesthetic learner. For the autistic child, the other senses can leak over into the kinesthetic realm. We even have terms for this: to be "hit by the smell," "an assault on the senses," "to touch with a look," "the taste was so spicy it burned." These are just some examples of how we can imagine the experience of sensory experiences bleeding into each other.

There are so many examples of what happens for the autistic person when sensory input gets to be too much and it becomes sensory overload. Imagine what it feels like at a loud concert venue, when the sound becomes so overwhelming that you almost stop taking in any information through any other senses. It is easy to understand why these events produce such intense visual displays at the same time – the auditory assault has to be matched by an equally intense visual assault or they would cancel each other out. I once attended a circus performance in an outdoor tent, with multiple acts performing in the ring at one time. The surrounding music was intensely loud, and the performers were jumping, swinging, flying, contorting, and climbing. An autistic boy, who looked like he was about ten years old, appeared to be completely flipping out. He was yelling loud enough to overcome the music, he was rocking and banging, and it looked at first like he was melting down. I started watched more closely because the mother took all this behavior in her stride and did not seem distressed by it. I gradually recognized that he was rocking and bouncing in a direct response to the movements of the performers, and that his voice, while incredibly loud, was matched to the music. He couldn't just take in the sensory overload of the sights and sounds, but by conquering them with his own movements and sounds, it appeared that he was able to "coordinate" the sensory assault.

Kinesthetic language is essential to the learning process. Students coming to my office for tutoring often need to set themselves up with a kinesthetic outlet so they can calm that sensory channel enough to open up another, such as the auditory or visual channel, that could be needed for the academic work at hand. I have balls or twirly chairs to sit on, fiddleables to fiddle with, a tray of kinetic sand that they can use for just touching, etc. I have a small couch with very soft pillows, and they are welcome to sit on the floor if that helps initially. The student can use any of these options to calm the kinesthetic nerves and listen more carefully to the reading or whatever school content we need to work on that day. Conversation is also easier if the child's kinesthetic needs are met first.

Autistic students are prone to sensory overload, so understanding and respecting this fact is essential to their sense of wellbeing. Monitoring how many sensory channels they are required to have open at any given time helps maintain balance. In the classroom, it supports learning if we can find alternative ways to communicate information and not rely too heavily simply on auditory commands and messages. Parents and teachers can write things down, look at the child/student, and point to what they should do, and/or use hand gestures for repeating messages.

One mother described how her son could get frustrated trying to communicate verbally and preferred to draw what he was trying to say. She kept a dry erase board in the house, so he could access that and communicate through this kinesthetic drawing activity whenever he needed. There were times when she would also send messages back to him this way, and he could deal with them in his own time. Other times, he might be able to communicate through verbal language, but only if he was spinning something in his fingers, or fiddling with something in order to keep the touch channel open.

In the previous chapter, we heard how Michael speaks what we now understand as kinesthetic language:

He uses touch for communication of thoughts or feelings instead of finding appropriate words or functional language. He flicks his brother's hair to convey disappointment, frustration, or disapproval, and rubs or plays with his brother's hair to share affection, agreement, or to get attention. He rubs my hair or his teacher's hair to find solace or security. His clothes can't have any tags or seams that are bumpy, and the waists of his clothing need to have the correct amount of pressure. He would rather wear clothes two or more sizes too small to achieve the preferred compression tension. He wants fabric to cover his arms at all times regardless of temperature. He throws himself into furniture, floors, etc. as a way of seeking feedback.

What might appear as a random gesture, thoughtless movement, or unintended contact might, in fact, be targeted and intentional communication from the autistic child to others. The fine differentiation between flicking his brother's hair to convey disappointment and rubbing hair to show affection requires some refined translation skills on the part of the teachers and parents. In this case, siblings also need to be taught how to speak these autistic languages, since they are the ones who live together with an autistic sibling day in, day out.

Sensory language

Sensory language includes all our senses. The language of touch is engaged when we touch soft/hard, wet/dry, smooth/rough, etc. The languages of smell and taste tell us if something is sweet, sour, bitter, or salty. Our smell and taste essentially tell us if something is good or bad. The sense of warmth tells us when we are too hot, too cold, or just right. It is our sensory language that establishes and communicates an overall sense of wellbeing.

Sensory language becomes a combined language. All of the languages discussed so far have a sensory component, so sensory language can be understood to be a blend of all the other languages. It is the language of interaction, recurring patterns, and structured systems. It could be said that there is an element of an "autistic learning cycle" expressed through sensory language, when the different languages come together. One adult describes this as the pattern of her day. She likes it best when she can not only organize, but also predict, what is going to happen in a given situation or in the entire day. As an example, she is sensitive to social interactions so she prefers to be given a specific task to do during the social event that prevents her from having to respond to a variety of interactions. Social interactions and events like this fall outside her normal daily routine, so they need to be well planned. She can get her regular daily patterns in place easily enough, but these extra events always hold the potential for sensory overwhelm and social overload, and therefore are prone to end in meltdowns. Once the overwhelm or overload gets established, there is almost no other way out than to melt down. As an adult, she has learned to set up her situation to avoid the overwhelming moments, and has become more skilled at speaking a sensory language. She did not learn this fast or easily, though, so we can start teaching sensory language and coping skills to children.

One helpful tool in teaching sensory language is modeling and structure. Even our adult found safety in structure, so children are very likely to feel safe in a predictable structure. Once a pattern is modeled and established, it is very difficult for an autistic child to have to adapt to changes. Change is not the friend of autistic children or adults. Change cannot be avoided entirely through life, so learning to speak the language of change is important, but an autistic child learns this language slowly, over a long period of time. In this regard, there is no such thing as quick change. It is possible to teach strategies that will help a child or adult adapt when change is forced on them, and then to understand as they get older that they might get better at setting personal strategies when they are confronted by the stress of change. The predictability of the senses can help set up recognizable patterns here, and if change is necessary, it can help to start with a familiar, recognizable sensory experience. For example, before a new food is introduced, be sure to have a familiar one available. Then bring the new food back into that context frequently enough for it to become a known and recognized food. When introducing a new activity, have a familiar sensory experience available (the feel of familiar clothes, familiar smells, or preferred colours). What becomes familiar to the child's sensory language is always a good place to start when introducing change. The familiar is a place of strength and confidence, so it is the perfect place to be when embarking on the scary, unfamiliar journey of change.

4

Unlocking the Executive Functions through the Autistic Access Points

---

Key points

- Autistic Access Points, or AAPs, are the ingredients or tools needed for understanding and using executive function, tailored specifically for the individual with autism.

- AAPs offer a foundation for the autistic person for interpreting, processing and understanding the world with flexibility.

- AAPs might work very differently for the autistic person than they do for the non-autistic person, but once understood, it is much easier to support, and provide validation for, the autistic person's perceptions and experiences.

- AAPs can be used to build a strong and effective executive "toolbox" of executive skills.

The AAPs discussed in this chapter provide ways to make executive function more accessible. Executive functions are complex capacities for everyone, and it is unrealistic to expect that anyone can master these functions without some help. The ultimate goal is to acquire successful executive capacities, and AAPs are offered here as support for this executive skill development. They are entry or access points, but could also be referred to as tools or ingredients.

The ingredients are similar to the ingredients a cook needs to be familiar with in order to choose how to combine the ingredients available for the chosen result. Flour, eggs, and milk can become a sweet dessert, a savory dish, a type of bread, etc. Flour might be used in many different dishes, but the cook must understand the nature of this ingredient in order to use it effectively. This analogy can go on and on, but the basic principle is that using salt as an ingredient, for example, is a good thing. It can make flavors taste better, even in sweet dishes. But too much salt is both unpleasant and unhealthy, while too little salt results in a boring, flat taste. Since the ultimate goal of our executive function is to achieve a state of coherence, it is important to know how to both identify and then use the ingredients at the right level and in a good balance. The goal is essentially to use the right ingredient for the right reason.

The ingredients described in my first book on executive function (Moraine 2012) were:

- relationships

- strengths and weaknesses

- self-advocacy

- review/preview and mental image

- whole to the parts and parts to the whole

- motivation and incentive

- rhythm and routine

- implicit and explicit.

These ingredients provide a way of understanding the basic tools or skills needed for effective use of our executive functions. How the autistic person uses these "ingredients" is quite different, in most cases, from how they are used by the non-autistic person, so I found that I needed to translate each one for the autistic students to make them more recognizable and more accessible. My question was, "How does the autistic student access these ingredients?" That simple question led me to re-name these ingredients in this book as Autistic Access Points.

AAPs are tools for understanding and using executive function, tailored specifically for the individual with autism. They offer ways that help the autistic person to create contact with ideas, space, people, animals, etc. Autistic individuals can often feel isolated, and are frequently offered only "non-autistic" ways to interact with the world. Understanding the AAPs will ease that sense of isolation. The AAPs will help those with autism establish predictability in their lives through detecting and creating recurring patterns to rely on as well as help direct and structure attention. Ideally, understanding the AAPs will offer a foundation for the autistic person for interpreting, processing and understanding the world with flexibility.

Relationships

Jimmy walks into the classroom early on a Monday morning. He is the first to arrive and I smile and greet him. I know better than to touch him right away, so I walk closer to him and stop before I cross that line of acceptable closeness. I start to inquire about his weekend, but he is looking around and is clearly not comfortable with something. His hand starts to flap, his begins to twirl his head back and forth, and I can see an outburst bubble up, ready to blow. In my early days of teaching autistic children, I might have thought I had done something wrong. Maybe I had spoken too soon, or walked too close to him before he was ready. But that was not the problem. Jimmy was not interested in the fact that I was even in the room; he did not even recognize me as part of the architecture. He had noticed that the desks had been moved into new positions, and there were new materials on the walls. The architecture of the room had changed, and he was used to making his relationships to space, not to people. I stepped back, let him go to his desk, and gave him time to re-adjust his sense of order with the new desk placement. He continued to flap his hands, but gradually his head tipping slowed down, and he was able to re-adjust to the new configuration. It took a little longer before he was able to sit down, but eventually he made the adjustment to the new layout.

Jimmy is just one example of how the autistic person tends to make a relationship with space before people. It can be very upsetting to enter a space, expecting one kind of configuration, and suddenly it is different. For Jimmy, the space no longer matched the picture of layout and order that was in his head. A verbal warning of the change may have helped a bit, but it might just as easily have triggered a stronger reaction, and Jimmy might have refused to even enter the room.

Liam, the young student who was so interested in animals, makes his relationship to ideas before he will make a relationship to a person. He finds his comfort in the use of pragmatic/practical language. He likes his animal books of facts, and can talk for hours about how fast a cheetah runs, or where bald eagles build their nests. His vocabulary is immense, yet if you listen carefully to what he is saying, it is all idea- or fact-based. He will gladly engage in a conversation, but becomes very upset if you ask him to engage on a personal level. A conversation with Liam sounds like this:

"Good morning, Liam. How are you this morning?"

"Did you know that spotted salamanders stay underground during the day and only come out at night to feed?"

"I didn't know that, Liam. Do you like salamanders?"

"They are very hard to see, mostly because they only come out at night."

"Have you ever had a pet salamander?"

"They eat insects, worms, slugs, spiders, and millipedes."

"If you had a pet salamander, would you be willing to feed it with insects and worms?"

"Salamanders are amphibians, and so are warty newts. Warty newts are even harder to find. They live in Europe and are nocturnal like salamanders, but they are different. They will also eat underwater and on land. The salamander will only eat on land."

Liam is verbose and very comfortable in the world of pragmatic language. He likes facts based on realistic descriptions. Liam can hold a conversation like this for hours, but his ability to engage in a relationship with either an adult or his classmates is very limited. He does not directly answer the questions he is asked, but proceeds following his own direct line of thought. It might sound like a conversation between Liam and me, but in reality, he could have had that same conversation completely alone. Jimmy is less of a talker, and his stress in any given situation shows more easily in his movements and his noises. In order for either Jimmy or Liam to learn how to make relationships with people rather than things, they have to begin where they are comfortable. With Liam, I introduced the idea that we could talk about his animals for a specific amount of time, and then he would have to engage in a conversation that did not include the animals for a brief time. In these moments I would make one personal comment, ask one question, and share a bit about what we would learn that day. I never tried to take advantage of our arrangement and push him too hard or too fast according to my standards. I always acknowledged that he had worked well that day or engaged in a good conversation, and then he could go back to his comfort zone in pragmatic language with his ideas and thoughts about animals.

Jimmy needed time to make his own relationship with the space and any changes in that space. I would gradually introduce a person-to-person conversation with him; I started by coming near his desk, and after a moment of adjustment, would place my hand on his desk. This was as electric a sensation for him as if I had touched his face. I let my hand rest on his desk for a time, said something personal to him that reflected a normal conversation, and then moved away and let him adjust. Gradually, over time, this show of understanding and respect for his ability to make a relationship with space allowed him to begin to trust me, and slowly made it possible for him to respond to me as a person.

These are just two types of examples that demonstrate the remarkable and highly developed ability of an autistic person to easily make a relationship to ideas or space, and how important it is to slowly and respectfully cultivate the ability to make a relationship to another person.

Strengths and weaknesses

The conversation around strengths and weaknesses in education typically revolves around learning styles and types. Do you learn best through visual, auditory, or kinesthetic modes? Are you better at language arts, or math? Are you naturally good at sports or better at building things? These types of questions are common for non-autistic students, but they are not that helpful with autistic students because the autistic person differentiates based on different criteria. Instead of asking autistic students if they are visual, auditory, or kinesthetic learners, it is better to observe in what way they process visual, auditory, or tactile sensory experiences. If an autistic student were highly sensitive to noise, for example, then any auditory learning would need to be moderated or modulated to meet his or her threshold of auditory tolerance. That student might be very capable of processing auditory or spoken language, and might be an excellent auditory learner, but processing the sensation of sound might pose enough of a challenge to block auditory learning. So, in this example, the autistic student might answer the question, "Are you good at learning through listening or learning because you hear it?" with the simple answer that they don't like noise. Observing the autistic student's response to the environment, and specifically to the manner in which the autistic person processes sensory input, may be a more effective approach to getting these questions answered than asking the question directly.

The environment plays a strong role in affecting an autistic person's sense of his or her strengths and weaknesses. An autistic student who is excellent in math might struggle with decoding, reading, and written expression. This is a common scenario for students, but the difference for the autistic student lies in how the environment is set up to support or hinder his or her specific strengths in math or weaknesses in language arts.

Joan has come in for her usual tutoring session. Her mom asked if we could work on her math homework if there was time at the end of our session. Joan's math is an area of academic strength, but the class was learning new concepts in fractions and her mom wanted to be sure she had sufficient understanding. Joan started working on her language arts; spelling was the specific focus at that moment, when we ran into a concept that was a "rule breaker." Joan became irritated, then distressed, and then started self-calming behaviors. She started to rock, made little murmuring sounds, and kept trying to find ways to deal with these breaks in the patterns. I brought the spelling session to a close, and turned to her math instead, hoping it would lessen her distress and remind her of one of her strengths. But it didn't work. Despite the fact that she was naturally good at math, Joan was not

> *flexible enough in that moment to be objective about her strengths and weaknesses. She was still affected by the experience of being upset at the rule-breaking word, which colored all other experiences that followed. In this situation, it did not matter that she had strengths and weaknesses; she was not able to access them so they did not provide an AAP for her. She was simply engulfed by a roadblock.*

This story highlights the problem of AAPs, namely, that they do not always provide access. In the language of the previous book (Moraine 2012), this story illustrates the difficulty of using the ingredients, because at any given moment the autistic individual might be blocked from both their strengths and weaknesses, so it is not possible to use these ingredients or to access their individual capacities when these points of entrance are blocked.

Introducing an action that can serve as a "re-set" button will be more effective than forcing the issue of math or spelling. With Joan, I suggested taking a short break, moved over to sit next to her rather than across from her, removing myself from her line of vision. I knew that I had a math game she liked to play, so I suggested a 5-minute game, and she willingly accepted. This made it possible for her to re-group, re-set, and begin again. At other times, I have suggested that Joan look up a specific item on the computer. Computers are predictable and familiar to her, and therefore comforting. Once she was calm, we could return to the math lesson without resistance.

Self-advocacy

Self-advocacy sounds like a great idea, but it is difficult to achieve. Advocacy means supporting a cause or an idea. According to the definition on the Wrightslaw website:

> Self-Advocacy is learning how to speak up for yourself, making your own decisions about your own life, learning

how to get information so that you can understand things that are of interest to you, finding out who will support you in your journey, knowing your rights and responsibilities, problem solving, listening and learning, reaching out to others when you need help and friendship, and learning about self-determination.[1]

This is a practical, encompassing definition, and on the Wrightslaw website you can learn what their youth ambassadors have to say about self-advocacy. I have asked parents and teachers if they personally feel able to self-advocate, and the responses I get are revealing. They carefully pick and choose the situations they find conducive to their "self-advocacy voice." A teacher might not stand up for a personal need at school because of concerns that the principal or head teacher will not understand. The teacher may fear retribution or is concerned about consequences if he or she speaks up for what they need rather than simply accepting the working situation without question. Concerns about blowback exist in most working environments, so self-advocacy is generally not encouraged in the adult world. In personal relationships, fear of not being understood or heard can prevent us from speaking up. When parents do not agree on how to raise their children, one parent frequently acquiesces and pulls back from the discussion, letting the stronger voice dominate. The quieter parent decides not to advocate for their point of view, pointing to an aspect of self-advocacy that is not discussed very often.

We need to be clear about the power paradigm before we rush in to teach self-advocacy. Does the student feel a basic level of respect coming from those around him or her? Do we grant the student the power to have a voice? When we give our students a voice, we give them the power to choose from the available options. The following is a very simple example of the power of self-advocacy.

---

1   See www.wrightslaw.com/info/self.advocacy.htm

Brett entered the classroom every morning slowly and cautiously, yet mildly eager to learn. He was extremely intelligent, and learning gave him pleasure. In the early days of the school year, the teacher was attempting to set some easy-to-follow rules and expected routines. She knew how important routines were, so she set up the classroom day with clearly identifiable routines at frequent points in the day. The morning routine was easy, she thought, because it involved simply hanging one's jacket or coat on the hook, and placing the backpack on the shelf. She was thoughtful and wanted to keep it simple for her students. Brett, however, took issue with this.

> *"Good morning, Brett. Please hang up your jacket and go to your desk."*
>
> *"No."*
>
> *"No? No what?"*
>
> *"No, I won't hang up my jacket."*
>
> *"Brett, that is the class routine. Everyone hangs up their jacket before going to their desk."*
>
> *"No."*
>
> *"Brett, are you refusing to do what you are asked to do?"*
>
> *"No."*
>
> *"Then please hang up your jacket and go to your desk."*
>
> *"No."*

This conversation could go on for a while, but the point is that the teacher kept responding to Brett's "No" as if it was a statement of defiance against her authority. The real message behind Brett's "No" was something quite different. The conversation could have gone in a completely different direction.

"Good morning, Brett. Please hang up your jacket and go to your desk."

"No."

"No? No what?"

"No, I won't hang up my jacket."

"OK, is there a reason you do not want to hang it up?"

"I would have to take it off to hang it up."

"Do you want to leave your jacket on?"

"Yes."

"Can you share with me why you want to leave your jacket on?"

"I can't stand the feeling of air moving on my arms and I have a t-shirt on today. I will get distracted by that feeling of the air on my arms. I want to keep my jacket on."

"Now I understand. Thank you for telling me. Please go to your desk and get ready to start."

Brett just self-advocated, and when the adult listened to him, it worked out very well. This teacher found other times in the day to support the students with routine, and Brett was comfortable with all of them, and he did keep his jacket on throughout the day. Self-advocacy is often most successful when expressed in these small ways all day long. When the teacher began to engage in a power play, Brett had no chance at self-advocacy. When the teacher asked a small question, then really listened for the answer, it was suddenly not a big issue and Brett was allowed to go through his day without being tormented by air blowing on his arms.

Earlier, we identified that the autistic person makes relationships with space or ideas before establishing a relationship with other people. In the case of self-advocacy, the level of self-knowledge needed to self-advocate is based on having a sufficiently strong relationship with oneself so that it is possible to first identify one's needs, then to speak up for those needs to another person. This is simply a double-whammy of difficulty for an autistic person who finds making relationships with people difficult at the best of times. Then we expect them to speak up and self-advocate in situations that are likely stressful and challenging. In the first example with Brett, his stress level was increasing with every response that sounded like he was going to be forced to take his jacket off. In the second example, his anxiety and stress remained very low, so when he was asked to share his reason, he hadn't shut down his systems in self-defense, and could give a pretty clear and easy answer.

When a student cannot give a clear response as Brett did in the second example, it falls on the adult to translate by interpreting behaviors and listening to the unspoken words. Translating comes naturally to some people, but for others it is simply not easy, so interactions end up as a power struggle that does nothing to enhance or encourage self-advocacy.

Review/preview and mental image

In my experience, engaging in review and preview is the single most important activity that builds and strengthens executive function. Review is the act of reflecting on previous thoughts, emotional experiences, and actions or events. Preview is the ability to look into the future, picture what is coming, and prepare or plan one's actions accordingly. We can all do this in some measure, though it is much easier for some than others. Our review and preview takes place unconsciously most of the time, and is used in the most mundane, daily activities. When we get dressed in the morning, we put on our clothes, and then after we are finished, we put on our shoes. We can quickly, and unconsciously, review our previous experiences with putting on our clothes. It worked well to wait until the end and put the shoes on last. Assessing the current situation, also unconsciously, it makes sense to plan to dress in the same order today because it has worked before. Review – what did I do last time I was in this situation? Preview – if I do it that way again it will probably work well again. So the plan to get dressed in the same order can be implemented, and the shoes come last.

This is an easy example, but what happens when the autistic child does not experience the link between one experience and the other? It might work with getting dressed if he or she gets dressed in the same room at the same time every day. What happens when you go on vacation and this child needs to get dressed in a different room, with different clothes? Suddenly, there is no picture to call up in review, because this room is new. The most important thing about getting dressed at home is that the room is the same, and getting dressed is of secondary importance. The primary relationship is formed with the environment, not the activity.

Parents and teachers have excellent opportunities to help children learn to review and preview. It is done in a thousand little ways all through the day, but if specific time is taken to practice, it can help a great deal. Teachers can start the lesson with a short review of the previous lesson and a few words about what will be taught in the present lesson. At the end of the lesson, teachers could provide a short review of the lesson, and a brief preview of what the student can expect the next day. In terms of time, the teacher might spend only a minute engaging in this review and preview, but the long-term effect will be dramatic. Teachers have many, many other options for review and preview in specific situations, and can provide repeated opportunities for their students to model effective review and preview. Parents also have wonderful opportunities in the day for review and preview, particularly at night before the child goes to sleep. Reviewing the day before sleep is a perfect opportunity to review what happened during the day. This does not need to be in tremendous detail, but to just go backward through the day, noting the main events. Yes, backward is much better than starting at the beginning of the day and working forwards. Start at the end of the day, and "re-view" the events from the most recent to the furthest away in the day. Then, a quick preview, going forward through the coming day, will prepare the child for what is coming, and will make the events of the coming day seem familiar as they unfold.

Simple review and preview like this, either at home or at school, not only lays the groundwork for the development of executive functions, but it also builds the capacity to create mental images. Mental images are tricky because no two people create the same exact image. Read the word "apple." Every person reading this will form a different mental image of "apple," but that image will be connected by the concept "apple." There are a few characteristics that make all of those mental images true to the concept of the apple, but the color, size, lighting, setting, etc., will all be different. How does this work if a person speaks "pragmatic language"? Pragmatic language might drive the person to think of "apple" in exactly the same way every time. There is one mental image per concept. Visual language might cause us to create a mental image of the last apple we actually saw, or maybe a series of the most recent apples we saw. Emotional language might call to mind what the feelings are/were in relation to apples, kinesthetic language reminds of what the apple felt like or what the sensation of taste was, and sensory language might remind us that apples are on our banned list because they are too slippery, too sour, too crunchy, or too many different colors.

Mental images rule our world, though, and are not easily controlled from the outside. Not only are we hardly aware that we are forming mental images most of the time, but what makes us create associations and images is complex, mysterious, and highly individual. For many years, every time I stood at the kitchen sink to wash dishes, an image flashed in my mind of a girl I knew in fifth grade, and she was threading a needle. To this day, I have no idea if I ever saw this girl thread a needle in real life, but that image came completely unbidden to my mind whenever I washed dishes. I cannot make it stop before it happens, but I can shut it down quickly when it does come up because I do not need it.

Mental images can create an emotional response, a stress response, or a pleasant response. They are invisible to others, yet they are strong forces in behaviors. In the movie, *Temple Grandin*,[2] it showed how Temple looks at a gate, for example, and perceives the physics and architecture rather than a gate. I am quite sure I would have seen the wood, considered how it felt, looked for the latch, etc., but Temple saw what was behind the movement and the angles, and could imagine adding small changes to the construction to bring about a whole new utility. Her mental image of the gate was dramatically different from mine!

When autistic children become school-aged, and begin to learn to read, this issue of mental images becomes challenging. Remember the boy in the beginning of this book who created mental images of the book he was reading that included characters from a computer game, despite the fact that the book was set in the 1800s? We assess readers on their level of comprehension by asking questions about the reading passage. How much they can recall from the reading determines the comprehension score. These scores get a little skewed if the reader is creating different mental images than what is intended, and therefore remembers different facts from the reading. Reading comprehension is only partially based on recall of facts and "evidence" in the reading. Comprehension relies on the imaginations that are created while reading, images that form differently for every reader. Students are frequently asked to recall, re-state, and re-tell details from the reading passage, and comprehension assessments are based on such recall. For the autistic reader, mental images are based on their autistic subjectivity, so their interpretations are based on their autistic languages that are, in turn, based in the individual's forms of perception. This is one good reason not to assume that you

2   *Temple Grandin.* Warner Bros. 2010.

and the autistic student are forming the same, or even related, mental images of the same reading passage. Comprehension is also dependent on the reader making connections to previous knowledge, and those connections might also work very differently for the autistic reader. It is simply a good idea to engage with the autistic child as they are learning to read to understand what mental images they are forming, and add important adjustments or additional information.

Whole to the parts and parts to the whole

Each one of us has a tendency to see the world from a whole to the parts or parts to the whole perspective. For example, this becomes very evident when students are asked to write essays. Teachers generally instruct students to choose a topic and to write an outline. Then they are asked to write a thesis statement, an introduction, and as they write key thoughts for each paragraph, they are asked to link each paragraph with a linking sentence. They write the conclusion and are finished. For some students, this is quite simply, a torturous process. Many hours are spent at night with parents and students in complete stress mode, little is getting written, and the student has no idea how to relate to the topic. Eventually, the essay gets written with heavy input from the parents, and the student still does not have a relationship with the essay. This whole to the parts approach does not work for this student.

A second scenario could be that of offering the student a second option, namely, to popcorn or brainstorm their ideas, and after getting all manner of ideas on paper, to look at them and see what themes and red threads or main ideas emerge. Then the organizing process begins, and only the ideas that relate to the theme make the cut, and something of an outline reveals itself. The student can then identify a working thesis statement, and just start writing. Once the ideas are all transferred over to the paragraphs, a conclusion becomes clear, and now it is time to return to the introduction and thesis statement, and to make adjustments. This is parts to the whole writing, and if the student thinks like this naturally, it will be easier for him or her to write independently in this mode.

Whole to the parts is difficult for most autistic individuals. Taking the example of Jimmy who entered the room and immediately became distressed because the details in the environment had changed, shows us how the experience of the parts has to be managed before the whole can be considered. The whole environment might be just fine, but if the single part that is important to that individual is out of order, or out of their version of order, it is distressing and distracting. It is the same for social interactions in that an autistic person might be so distracted by a look, sound, or touch that he or she is unable to process the whole person before that one detail is addressed. This need to process the parts before the whole can make the autistic person seem unsocial. While the autistic person is busy processing confusing sensory details, everyone else is frustrated because they are not engaging in socially acceptable interactions and responses. This often leads to the expectation that the autistic person is not social, and can inhibit his or her social growth and development. Our quick responses and reactions to the autistic person who is processing from the parts to the whole can prevent him or her from learning how to gradually build a whole picture.

Motivation and incentive

Motivation is individual, intrinsic, personal, and not easily changed by someone other than oneself. Motivation comes about through the merging of personal strengths and weaknesses, interests, knowledge, experiences, and feelings. In education, it is one of the most elusive areas of control, because we end up having to admit that we cannot motivate another person from the outside. We cannot control others through "motivating" them. We can help another person connect with his or her own motivation, but ultimately, motivation is a personal, private matter.

Incentive, on the other hand, is much less personal. It does affect us because we are vulnerable in the face of the punishment and reward system inherent in incentives. Incentive is the ultimate control panel, and in some cases, it is used as a weapon. At school and at home, we incentivize others through the threat of punishment, bad grades, or denied activities. In personal relationships, children can use incentive in social situations by making it clear that being accepted socially requires specific clothes, behaviors, video games, sports interests, etc. Oddly, it seems to be much easier to teach children how to use incentive as a power tool than it is to strengthen the core base of motivation.

In autism, these norms of motivation and incentive work a little differently. An autistic individual is motivated by the "autistic subjectivity" referred to in the beginning of this book. One way to understand this term is to think of it as the filter used to sort out all incoming and outgoing experiences. An autistic individual has a filter, akin to wearing prescription lenses that adjust perceptions by adjusting the filter. We can look through their lenses and get a sense for how they see the world, but it does not make us see things their way. We still need to employ empathy, instinct, respect, and knowledge in order to use this insight in a productive manner. This is an important point because it clarifies why we cannot change the other's motivation. How the autistic person sees and filters the world through autistic subjectivity creates the motivational base. The autistic individual is not easily susceptible to incentives because of autistic subjectivity, too. Their filter is not altered through incentives, rewards, or punishments. So many parents and teachers have come to this same conclusion through difficult experiences of trial and error. It does not help to threaten and punish an autistic child for having a reaction due to sensory overload, for example. No amount of threat or punishment will lessen the overload or change the reaction. Taking the triggers away, lowering the threat level, creating an environment where the overload can deflate, these are all good options, but just throwing incentives around pollutes the atmosphere for an autistic child.

Rhythm and routine

What is the difference between rhythm and routine? This is a tricky question, mainly because we are more accustomed to thinking of our daily routines. Rhythms are more frequently associated with yearly rhythms or seasonal rhythms, when the same season comes around rhythmically every year, yet no two seasons are exactly alike. Birthdays also come around every year on the same day, yet the same birthday does not come around twice. Routines do repeat exactly, though. The order of how we do things might be the same exact routine every day. The order and routine of getting dressed, eating meals, doing daily chores can be very predictable and very patterned. The rhythm of the day might be a bit different each day, while the routines within that day might be exact replicas of previous days.

Rhythm and routine are related to practice and repetition. Practice, for example, is when the student practices the four or five pieces of music to prepare for the next lesson. Repetition is when one specific skill is practiced to gain complete mastery. An example could be practicing a musical scale over and over and over until it can be played exactly that way each time. This kind of repetition establishes muscle memory and can be applied to any activity that is repeated so many times that it is an established memory. Repetition can be used in learning to write, learning to play an instrument, or learning to play a sport. Rhythm will be used when learning the skill for the first time, for example, through the rhythm and flow of the pencil when forming letters, in learning to hear and play the melody, in getting a feel for throwing or kicking.

Routines are important to autistic children and adults. Routines are predictable, consistent, and repeatable, and therefore provide security. Routines are not transitional, which means that they are not easily adapted as transitions. Transitions, by their very nature, require flexibility and adaptability. Routines protect us from flexibility, and provide tremendous security. They can appear in every area of life, from daily activity routines to routines in thinking. One mother described how her son needed to be the one who turns the lights and electronics on and off. If someone else turns the lights off, it does not register for him, and he will repeatedly question if it was done. Another child has a specific routine for preparing for school – each item must be put in the backpack in a certain order, clothes put on in a certain order, and everything picked up to go to the bus in a certain order. These routines provide the basis of security, and disturbances in the routine disturb the child's sense of safety.

Routines do get disturbed upon occasion, though, and when an autistic person does not get sufficient warning or preparation time, it can cause outbursts or meltdowns. Using review and preview as a way of strengthening flexibility is an excellent tool. If a child is prepared in advance for a change in routine, it can potentially prevent that meltdown. The evening review and preview time can be used to prepare for changes in a daily schedule, such as a change in the school day schedule that can be discussed the night before. If it is not possible to give advance warning the night before, previewing what is going to happen soon is still important for those children who rely on routine for safety and comfort. The story I used in *Helping Students Take Control of Everyday Executive Function* (Moraine 2012) is a relevant description of how important it is to prepare students for what is coming, whether the child is autistic or not.

A powerful example of the value of preview came one day from a wonderful little boy named Duncan. I was teaching second grade, it was early in the school year, and it was early in the morning. We had been working for under an hour, and I was in the middle of teaching the day's lesson. Suddenly, there was an ear-splitting, heart-stopping scream in the room. I stopped in mid-sentence and slowly scanned the room to see where this unearthly sound came from and who had made it. Eventually, my eyes settled on Duncan, who was sitting there looking incredibly distressed. I went to him, invited him to join me just outside the classroom door on the deck, and sat down quietly next to him. We sat there for a moment, and then I said, "Can you tell me about it?"

"I just had to do that," he said.

"Ah," I said, "can you tell me more?"

Then Duncan said that I hadn't told him what was coming that day, and that I had to tell what was coming that day. So I agreed to do this better in the future and when we came back in the room, he settled quietly down at his desk. From then on, I always told the students the very first thing in the morning what we were going to be doing that day, and I told them that if any changes came up in the course of the day, I would let them know right away. I also started previewing the next day just before the students went home. Duncan was happy with this arrangement, the other students did not seem to mind hearing about the day's schedule in advance, and life continued quite happily in the classroom. The daily schedule was always on the board, but for Duncan, the visual schedule did not satisfy him as much as the verbal accounting. I credit Duncan with teaching me a valuable lesson about the value of preview, and have been more mindful and respectful of it ever since.

This example is especially interesting because Duncan does not have autism, yet changes in the routine of his school day were simply distressing and anxiety-producing. A short preview of the day eased his worries, and he was available for learning; it did not take much effort to make a very big difference. Similarly, preview and review will help the autistic child who is dependent on his or her routines, and while simply previewing possible changes might not prevent all the meltdowns caused by routine changes, it is a way to gradually teach more tolerance for change.

Routines also get established in thought processes in specific subject areas. One fifth grade student was struggling with spelling, and kept mixing up the letters "n" and "m." He was a very smart student, could remember all the verbal content from class, but I noticed early in the school year that once he thought he understood something, it was very hard to correct any misunderstanding. An example of this was the fact that he was convinced his former teacher (from several years prior to fifth grade) had told him that the "m" was an "n," and vice versa. The fact that this was not correct did not sway him; he was sure that his former teacher had said this, so it was his firm conviction. He was set in his way of thinking, and was similarly set in his way of doing certain things. His routines showed up both in his thinking and in his actions. Yet this same child was one of the most creative and out-of-the-box thinkers I have ever come across.

I had been telling stories from Greek mythology and asked the students to find a way to re-tell a story in their own way. This same student got a large piece of paper, a dark blue crayon, and started scribbling the entire page full of solid dark blue color. I did not say anything about this, but watched him with interest. He did not say anything, either, but just scribbled his paper blue. Then he took a handful of clay and waited his turn. When I called on him, he took my chair, put it on top of my desk, laid the blue paper on the floor in front of the desk, and climbed up on top of the chair. From that vantage point, he re-told the story of Theseus, son of King Aegeus, who promised to sail home, and if all was well, he would hoist the white flag so his father could see from the top of the cliff that he was coming home alive, but that if he had been killed, the crew was to fly a black flag. The king was watching from the top of the cliff, saw the ship, and did not know that the black flag had been hoisted in error, so he thought his son was dead. The king threw himself off the cliff in anguish. At this point, the student took the clay that he had formed roughly into the shape of a person, held it high, and let it drop with a big splat, into the "sea" on the blue paper. The room was silent. It was a brilliantly simple re-telling of a story with every nuance depicted in the most simple, yet visual manner. This was the same student who usually could only re-tell or repeat what he had learned in a kind of routine manner. Through an imaginative, artistic re-telling of the story, he was freed from routinized thinking. He was able to engage in his executive development through activities of this nature, reviewing and previewing stories, expressing what he had learned through visible actions and pictures. Over time he became more flexible, imaginative, and able to initiate his own thinking, and ultimately direct his own attention more freely. This gave me great insight into the option for students to express themselves through art, drawing, painting, and even music, as a way to be free of the repetitive necessity of routine.

Implicit and explicit

In everyday life, we all have experiences that are explicit. These experiences should be clear and obvious, and most of the time we all agree on the explicit things in life. In the movie about Temple Grandin referred to earlier, there was a scene where Grandin drove up to a gate and the person driving the truck saw a gate. That was expected, and obvious – or it was explicit. The driver saw the gate, and the movie viewer also was expected to see the gate. The movie depicts Grandin seeing a series of pulleys, levers, and relationships of movement instead of simply seeing the gate. The gate was not explicit to her in this scene, but instead, what became obvious to her was what lay behind the scene of the gate, how it worked, and what could be done to change it. The physics and mechanical workings of the gate remained implicit to the others. In this example, one kind of perception took things at face value, seeing the explicit facts. Another kind of perception saw the principles and physics behind the scenes. The implicit became explicit through autistic subjectivity.

This might be what is happening to autistic perception more often than not. In school, students are asked to read literature, and based on their reading comprehension, they are expected to answer questions, write essays, produce book reports, etc. As the student reads the story, are pictures forming for that student that relate to the explicit information in the book, or are different pictures forming that are explicit only to that student? The student might not be able to answer the obvious questions after reading because those are not the obvious pictures that formed for him or her. It is important to refrain from making assumptions about what might be implicit or explicit to the autistic student. As teachers and parents we often set our expectations based on what we perceive or assume. We set the standards based on our systems of perceptions, but every time we are able to hold back and ask what the student sees or experiences first, we will come closer to being able to use their manner of processing as an effective AAP. Processing information through implicit and explicit channels is a requirement for our executive functions; it is one of the ways we get information to our executive brain. As an AAP, the important thing to remember is that we do not all process implicit and explicit the same way.

AAPs are the ingredients or tools needed in order to gain access to the executive brain and executive functions. They might work very differently for the autistic person than they do for the non-autistic person, but once these are understood, they are much easier to support, and provide validation for the autistic person's perceptions and experiences. In the next chapter, these AAPs are referred to again, and applied to the everyday experiences of executive function.

5

Executive Functions in the Autistic Experience

Key Points

- The eight skills of executive control are: attention, memory, organization, planning, inhibition and initiative, flexibility, control of behavior and emotion, and goal setting.

- Executive functions can be made coherent for the autistic person when their experiences are comprehensible, meaningful, and manageable (see Chapter 2).

It might be unexpected to some readers that this chapter comes relatively late in the book, since most written works on the theme of executive function deal immediately and directly with the more traditionally named executive functions, and do not address the skills and developmental milestones that lead up to using our executive functions. Surprisingly, there is no single, definitive, scientifically proven list of what the executive functions are and are not. Different researchers and authors will use their own formulation or vocabulary to define and describe the executive functions. These terms are also constantly evolving, as more research and more experiences are gathered. This can be confusing to parents, who more frequently have to just deal with the manifestation of the behaviors that result from the use of, or lack of, executive functions, and then find it particularly confusing when the concepts used by educators and other professionals to describe these behaviors are not consistent. The definitions offered are not confusing in themselves, but there are multiple definitions to choose from.

> Executive function is a set of mental processes that helps connect past experience with present action. People use it to perform activities such as planning, organizing, strategizing, paying attention to and remembering details, and managing time and space. (www.ldonline.org/article/24880/)

> The executive functions are a set of processes that all have to do with managing oneself and one's resources in order to achieve a goal. It is an umbrella term for the neurologically-based skills involving mental control and self-regulation.

> The executive functions all serve a "command and control" function; they can be viewed as the "conductor" of all cognitive skills.

> Executive functions help you manage life tasks of all types. For example, executive functions let you organize a trip, a research project, or a paper for school.

> Often, when we think of problems with executive functioning, we think of disorganization. However, organization is only one of these important skills. (www.ldonline.org/article/29122/)

There are other formulations and definitions that can easily be added to this list, but the executive function terms used in this book are consistent with the terms in the book *Helping Students Take Control of Everyday Executive Functions – The Attention Fix* (Moraine 2012):

- attention

- memory

- organization

- planning

- inhibition and initiative

- flexibility

- control of behavior and emotion

- goal setting.

Attention

The range of issues related to attention is at least as broad as the range of manifestations of autism. If we can speak about an "autism spectrum," we can surely speak about an "attention spectrum" as well. Just as no two individuals with autism are exactly alike, no two individuals have the same type of attention. Attention permeates most experiences of life – it is akin to breathing in that if we stopped paying attention for any significant amount of time, we would become unconscious. We all have attention, we all use attention, so the real question becomes, what are we paying attention to?

When students and parents come into my office, one of the first questions I frequently ask is, "What did you notice when you walked into this room?" I get some odd looks, and since I simply wait for an answer, the student usually starts telling me what he or she noticed. The parent is often quite surprised by the answers, and when I ask the parent to share what they noticed, the list is very different. The autistic student will answer in line with their verbal comfort level. When that comfort level is low, the answer might only be one or two things, but that still gives an excellent picture of what the student's attention takes in as important. I call this kind of attention the student's "passive" attention, what they notice or pay attention to naturally, with no one telling them they have to pay attention. The answers indicate if a person is more drawn to structure or form (size of room, shape, type of furniture); function of the room (desks, chairs, computers, white boards, clocks); visuals (window, light, color); auditory (sounds either inside or outside the room); touch (feel of the chair, furniture, writing supplies); people (who is or is not in the room, how many there are); social (what others are wearing, doing, saying), etc. It does not matter if the student only mentions one thing because I can always work with that one thing and gradually build on it to make a relationship with the student.

A conversation might go something like this:

"Eric, what did you notice when you first walked in the room?"

"I dunno." Pause. "Well, the ball."

"Do you mean this big ball or a different one?"

"Yeah, the big one."

"Do you know what that is for?"

"To sit on."

"Yes. Do you want to sit on it?"

"No."

"OK. Why not?"

"I would get dizzy and fall off."

"Do you want to try by holding onto the desk and seeing if you can balance?"

"Well, OK."

Eric then tries sitting on the ball, manages fine, and even smiles. It suits him. He does not have any trouble with balance, but he does have trouble with adjusting to new things quickly. He needed to be allowed to say "no" before he said "yes." I could hear that he was interested in the ball since it was the first, and only, thing he mentioned. Meanwhile, his mom is sitting there trying not to say anything because this is the boy who can bounce for hours on a trampoline, scoot madly along on a skateboard, and balance on top of the wooden fence in the back yard! Afraid he might fall off!! That sounds incredible to her.

"He never falls off anything, ever!" she declares.

"I am not surprised to hear that," I respond, "but I was pretty sure he was not worried about falling off. I do think he might have been worried about doing something new or different, in front of me, a new person in his life, in a new setting, facing an unknown set of expectations."

Eric's passive attention shifted over to his active attention as soon as I started speaking with him about the ball. Noticing the ball when he first walked into the room triggered all kinds on inner responses, known only to him, but he activated those responses when I began engaging him in conversation. This simple example of active and passive attention serves to point out the fact that our attention is constantly engaged in its passive mode, and shifts over to the active mode when something specific happens. We are all engaged with our active and passive attention all the time, so the real insight into attention is gained when we identify just how much time we spend in active mode and how much time we spend in passive mode.

Staying with Eric's example, as soon as we established his passive attention, I shifted over to a direct question related to the academic work he brought with him. His mother began to answer what it was and where to find it, but fortunately responded quickly to a slight gesture from me, indicating that I hoped she would let Eric answer on his own. As soon as she stopped, Eric noticed that the room was quiet and looked up at me. I repeated my request to show the work he had brought, and he pulled out his math sheets. Now he knows he is supposed to "pay attention" to me, but it is hard. He does not want to look me in the eye, and he feels a generalized sense of confrontation building. The first thing I do is to move my chair around to his side of the desk and sit down next to him. Now I have removed the major block – the requirement to pay full, face-on attention to me. The "frontal attack" has ended, so he can visibly relax. Sitting there, next to him, I wait a moment and see if he can initiate the next interaction and show me what he is working on in class, or show me his homework assignment. It takes a moment, but he starts to point to the place on the page, and shows me the problems he has for homework.

"Eric, show me how you do these kinds of problems."

"They are not hard, but the teacher won't let me do them the way I want."

"Show me the way you do them, the way you want to do them."

So Eric shows me how he works out the problem, and puts the correct answer down very quickly. His mind just worked at warp speed, accurately calculating the complex algebraic problem; he got the correct answer, but there was not a single step in that process written down on paper. I knew he did not use a calculator to get the answer, but the teacher would not know that.

"Eric, will your teacher accept this answer?"

"It's the right answer."

"I know that Eric, and you know that, but will the teacher accept this answer?"

"No."

"Why not?"

"Because I didn't show my work."

"Can you show your work?"

"Yes, of course."

"Why don't you?"

"It is like doing the same problem twice. I did it in my head, so why should I also write it down? I won't forget what I did. I can still see the problem written down there and know how to get the answer. Isn't it just extra work to write it down?"

With this statement, Eric just showed me how he processes his active attention. He looked at the problem, fully understood it, worked it out on his "internal blackboard," got the right answer and produced that answer on his page. Every step of that active attention process made sense to Eric. He was focused and clear during the whole activity of answering the math problem. The problem is that Eric will not be validated for using his active attention. Rather, he will be punished because his answer will be marked either fully wrong, or he will lose at least some credit for not showing his work. This is one clear area where an educational system is not receptive to individual learning styles. If Eric were allowed to work the way that suits him best, he would use his active attention to correctly compute these math problems in his head. When he did not understand the problem, then he could write it down, get a picture of how it works, and continue after that to work on his mental blackboard.

The requirement to process information in a specific way, and to "show your work" according to the teacher's standards, is common practice in many educational systems around the world. While I understand the need for this requirement from the teacher's perspective, it does not always have the desired effect on students' learning. From the perspective of active attention, or paying attention to that which we decide to pay attention to, Eric, and students like him, will pay active attention to these requirements until it becomes tedious, redundant, or even silly. At that point, the active attention shuts off and the passive attention takes over. The student will then appear to be engaged elsewhere, and their behavior will appear to go offline.

"Active" and "passive" attention is not just a childhood expression of attention. Throughout our lifetime, we all retain both active and passive attention. Our success in the workplace and in our adult relationships can often be traced back to what we actively and passively pay attention to. Active and passive attention also plays a strong role in any attention system that is diagnosed as ADHD.

ADHD is characterized by a pattern of behavior, present in multiple settings (e.g. school and home) that can result in performance issues manifesting in social, educational, or work settings. In the *Diagnostic and Statistical Manual of Mental Disorders: DSM-5* (APA 2013), symptoms are divided into categories of inattention, hyperactivity, and impulsivity that include behaviors like failure to pay close attention to details, difficulty organizing tasks and activities, excessive talking, fidgeting, or an inability to remain seated in appropriate situations. Symptoms must be present before the age of 12, and the DSM-5 takes adult experience into consideration. The threshold is set in the DSM-5 at meeting six of the possible symptoms rather than the previous level of five of the possible symptoms. Diagnosis is based on reports, observation, and self-reporting. There is no "blood test" for ADHD. The following are samples of the criteria used for diagnosis:

- persistent symptoms of inattention and/or impulsivity and hyperactivity

- onset of symptoms before age 7–12

- impairment in two or more settings (school, work, home)

- evidence of clinically significant impairment in social, academic, or occupational functioning

- the symptoms are not a result of other disorders.

The diagnosis of ADHD is also classified under one of these three types:

- ADHD *predominantly hyperactive-impulsive type*: this subtype should be used if the criteria are met if six (or more) symptoms of hyperactivity-impulsivity (but fewer than six of inattention) have persisted for at least six months. (Five symptoms are the threshold for adolescents and adults.)

- ADHD *predominantly inattentive type*: this subtype is used if the criteria are met for inattention but not for impulsivity/hyperactivity, and if six (or more) symptoms of inattention (but fewer than six symptoms of hyperactivity-impulsivity) have persisted for at least six months. (Five symptoms are the threshold for adolescents and adults.)

- ADHD *predominantly combined type*: this subtype should be used if the criteria are met for both inattention and impulsivity/hyperactivity and if six (or more) symptoms of inattention and six (or more) symptoms of hyperactivity-impulsivity have persisted for at least six months. (Five symptoms are the threshold in adolescents and adults.)

The medical management of ADHD is completely separated from the educational setting, although medical professionals will include reports from teachers and parents in the diagnostic process. Doctors can diagnose and possibly prescribe medication for ADHD. Educators and parents deal with the manifestation of ADHD on a daily basis as expressions of behavior, and can observe the impact of ADHD on learning, which is why it is important to understand these three types of diagnosis for ADHD. Children with both autistic characteristics as well as characteristics of ADHD will become adults with both of these characteristics. These are life-long issues, and the skills learned as a child can mature into effective skills that can be used by adults. When I work with adults, the most common comment I hear is, "I wish someone had taught me how to do this when I was younger." The issues related to attention and autism begin in childhood, and remain relevant core issues for a lifetime.

ADHD, predominately hyperactive-impulsive type, will manifest in very active, observable movement, speech, and behavior.

This ADHD type will have an increased or heightened need for movement and sensory stimulation, but might have a lower ability in processing. An example of this is the child who comes into the room, moving constantly, fiddling and twirling any possible object, hopping or bouncing on their toes, or filling up the space with chatter. The first tendency of the other people in the room is to start talking to this child, assuming that the movement and the child's chatter is an indication of their ability to process a lot of information in a short period of time. But the opposite is true; the child is moving, talking and fiddling as a way of keeping him or herself connected. I often describe attention as a light switch that, in the case of ADHD, is greasy. In this case, you turn on your attention, or your switch, and the switch almost immediately begins falling down into the off position. Then you need movement, talk, noise, or some sensory-based input to push the switch back up into the "on" position again, but since it is greasy, it begins nearly immediately to slowly fall down into the "off" position. Then comes the movement, noise, talk, etc., to get the switch back on. This becomes a nearly constant process for those with a "greasy" attention switch. This is an example of the person giving their active attention to the process of keeping the attention switch in the "on" position. The behavior looks very active and engaged, and the assumption is that this person is capable of processing a pretty active amount of information, so we might start talking to that person at a normal speed, maybe giving directions to something that needs to be done. This is where it all starts to fall apart. The person with ADHD hyperactive-impulsive type is very busy managing all of the sensory input that is coming in from their movements, chatter, or personal thoughts. Your input is not registering, and what you are saying to that person is arriving in the form of passive attention and is therefore being ignored because there is so much in the realm of active attention demanding focus. I have observed this kind of mis-match often occur between parents and students, and between teachers and students. The following are two different scenarios that describe this process in the classroom and at home.

Classroom

> *"Students, please get your notebooks ready for the daily drill. The drill is on the board, and today, please answer the questions in both mathematical notation and with a description of how you computed that problem. And John, please start getting ready and settle down."*

John does indeed look a bit squirrely, moving around in his seat, fussing with his binders, but he is also talking, though it is not clear who he is talking to.

> *"What notebook should I get out?"*

> *"I just told you, your daily drill notebook!"*

> *"Oh, OK. I think I have that here."*

John fusses some more with his books and papers, and meanwhile the other students are already finished with the first problem. John finds his drill notebook and takes another moment to dig around for a pencil, starts to gather his other notebooks to put them away, and by now the teacher is frustrated.

> *"John, really, for the amount of activity there has been at your desk this morning, you could have done the drill three times over!"*

Not only is John busy trying to deal with all the physical issues related to books, pencils, papers, and drill assignments, he now also has the added feeling of shame from being criticized by his teacher. What looks like productive activity in the form of moving papers and books around is really just sensory-based movement that serves the purpose of keeping John's attention switch "on." Just having his attention switch on does not automatically provide efficient processing of the attention tasks at hand. Put simply, outer activity is not a predictor for inner activity or effective processing.

The further behind John falls in the drill, the less productive his actions are. The more his inner attention is taken up with the feeling of shame, the less he is able to process information or interactions. It is only 5 minutes into the class, and he is already out of sync with the others, behind in his work, and his attention has been re-directed to dealing with the feeling of being ashamed. There is no easy recovery from a moment like this, so the usual trajectory is an escalation throughout the day of behaviors that get increasingly agitated, work that piles up, and a feeling of self-loathing that becomes entrenched.

Home

"Brendon, it is time to leave for school. We have to be in the car in 10 minutes!"

"Thanks, Mom, I will be right there."

"Be sure you have put everything you need in your backpack – your folder, homework, and pencil case were still on your desk this morning."

"Got it, thanks!"

Brendon goes over to his desk, but notices an open comic book on his chest of drawers before he gets there. That reminds him he was going to send his friend a message before school to set up a time to meet at recess. He looks around for his phone, remembers he left it in the playroom downstairs, and takes the stairs two at a time, swinging on the bannister as far as he can with each jump. He just broke his record by getting downstairs in five jumps instead of six! That score even beats his friends score who also got down in six jumps. His friend is much taller, so that is understandable, and makes his victory even more sweet. If he could repeat the feat, it would be make him confident that he could show *it off to his friend next time he came over. He races back upstairs and tries it again, and somewhere in the middle he notices that his mother is saying something.*

"Brendon, now we have about 2 minutes – are you all ready?"

"Almost, be right there!"

Yes, he made the new record a second time! Now he knows it is not a fluke. He can count it as many times as he wants, he will always be able to do the stairs in five jumps instead of six. That is so good, since five is a much better number. The number five gives him a warm, comfortable feeling that he likes very much. He looks up and notices he is in the playroom, but doesn't remember why he came. But he does remember breaking that record.

"Brendon, 30 seconds and I am going! Will you be in the car or are you missing school today?"

School!! That is what he should have been doing. He runs back up to his room, grabs his backpack and arrives at the door, just in time.

"Did you put your folder, homework, and pencil box in the backpack?"

Brendon races back upstairs, flustered now since he had forgotten the only things his mom asked him to do. He looks for them, remembers he forgot to get his phone from the basement, and thinks that one more try at his record sounds like fun. He streaks past his mom, grabs his phone, remembers he still doesn't have his papers from his room, runs up to get them, and with a smile he arrives six minutes late to go to school. His mom looks stressed and a bit angry, and he wonders why she is upset.

There is not an ounce of ill will in Brendon, but he is easily distracted and has difficulty with multi-step directions. He can think of the overview for one thing at a time, but as soon as he has to do one task in relation to another task, it begins to fall apart. He focuses on the activity he is currently engaged in, until something takes its place. That could be an event, someone speaking, a thought or idea, or even a sound. Once his line of focus shifts, he gives his full attention the new thought, feeling, or action. They each have equal pull for him, and he is generous with his attention when he switches. The problem lies in the fact that he does not remember the relevance or importance of the activity or action that he dropped to take up the new activity. Remember, this is not done intentionally, and Brendon will be very surprised to hear there was some expectation that he would follow through with his actions in order. First, load his backpack; second, get his phone; third, be ready at the care to go to school. These three main themes did pop up for him, just not in that order and they vanished when his thoughts jumped to whatever caught his attention along the way. He had not formed a clear mental picture of his first "task" and he did not make an agreement with his mom to do that one thing before any other. That opened the door for the many, charming distractions that prevented Brandon from picturing his notebooks and homework, picturing himself putting them in his backpack, and having them arrive safe and sound in the car to go to school. Making a strong mental image before an action can lead to much more successful actions overall.

ADHD hyperactive-impulsive type is easy to spot because the hyperactive-impulsive behaviors are generally visible. The behaviors can sometimes mirror the autistic behaviors of rocking, spinning, twirling, tapping, and chattering. One of the difficulties is that there might be behaviors that are similar to obsessive compulsive disorder (OCD) behaviors, Tourette-like tics, or anxiety. Fortunately, many more people now understand that autism can co-occur with ADHD, OCD, Tourette's, anxiety, and depression.

This is one of the facts that makes spotting ADHD Inattentive type a bit more difficult.

ADHD inattentive type is more difficult to observe because the inattention causes the student or adult to simply appear calm. In the classroom, these students fly well under the teacher's radar for long periods of time. The difficulty arises when the student is expected to follow directions and get started on the work, and it becomes clear they were not "tuned-in" enough to hear the instruction, and therefore have not processed the information, and are not engaged in the activity. They are not unwilling to do the work; they were simply "off-line" and did not know what was going on around them. In an adult situation, this is also problematic because the inattentive type of ADHD will cause the individual to miss instructions, miss steps in a process, and appear disinterested or irresponsible. The individual with autism might miss social signals at the best of times, and if there is an added diagnosis of ADHD inattentive type, it can look like intentional disregard for those around them. This kind of inattention, though, is no more intentional than breathing. ADHD hyperactive-impulsive type is also not intentional, but all of these attention types do need to be managed. An autistic individual can learn how to manage his or her attention in many ways using the same approaches that a non-autistic individual needs to use to manage attention.

The third type of attention is ADHD combined type. In this case, there are both manifestations of hyperactive-impulsive behaviors, as well as inattention. This can be the most confusing of all since the quiet behaviors of the inattentive type appear to be at odds with the hyperactive-impulsive type. These opposite behaviors require really flexible responses.

Jamie is a child who has a combined type of ADHD, and she is autistic. She becomes hyperactive and impulsive in social situations; the stimulation she feels when interacting with others, and the social expectations for specific responses make it very difficult for her manage her attention.

She actively tries to listen to her peers, and tries to figure out what the correct response should be. This causes some amount of agitation for her, because due to her autism, the situation has to be processed through her active attention and she has to try to remember the rules.

"When someone speaks to you, look at them."

"Take turns talking."

"Answer their questions."

"Ask about things they are interested in, don't just talk about what you are interested in."

"Don't jiggle around too much when you are talking with your friends."

This list could go on and on and on. Jamie is trying to actively remember it all, and it causes her to worry that she is forgetting something. In order to try to remember, she begins to rock ever so slightly. Then she starts twiddling with her fingers down by her side, and she gently flips the hair away from her face. Gradually, each of these movements grows in intensity, and before long, she is rocking and fidgeting and flipping her hair, and her friend finds a good reason to leave since it is disturbing to watch. Jamie gets agitated, goes after her friend, or gets upset with herself and a kind of depression begins.

In class, this Jamie is not present, but the inattentive Jamie is there, looking benign and sweet, quietly sitting at the edge of the room, causing absolutely no trouble. She misses the directions for the work related to the lesson; she forgets to write the homework down, and by the end of the week is in serious trouble with her parents and her teacher.

After the long school day, Jamie arrives home with her books and papers in disorder. The books she needs in order to get her homework finished are there today, but she does not remember to bring them home every day. Her mom gets home from work in time to ask her about her day, and looks into her backpack or book bag to see what is expected for homework. She tries to sort out the crumpled papers into useable piles. This is something Jamie's mom keeps meaning to teach Jamie how to do, but it would be just another task tacked onto an already exhausting day, so it is easier for Jamie's mom to just do it herself. Her mom asks Jamie to tell her what her homework is, but Jamie cannot come up with an answer. She has shut down most communication systems because she is just not able to keep processing her attention. Jamie is just too stressed by the processing demands to keep concentrating. She has already begun to self-soothe with her video game, and her mom decides to leave her alone for a while. Later in the afternoon, closer to evening, Jamie's mom remembers that they never did the homework so she calls Jamie in and asks again what the homework is, but naturally, Jamie still cannot remember. Her mom frantically searches for clues about the homework in Jamie's school bag, among her papers, and online. Eventually she pieces together what is expected and gives over the next hour to coaxing Jamie through her homework. Jamie is resistant and irritated. Her mom is frustrated and close to anger. It finally gets done, the books are closed with a bit of a slam, and Jamie is told to get ready for bed.

The next confrontation is imminent and predictable, as Jamie was pulled away from her own interests to face a recapitulation of the school day in the form of homework. Now, without being able to re-enter her self-chosen, soothing world, she is told to brush her teeth and get ready for bed. Her sensitivities kick in, and her mother's voice becomes too loud, the toothpaste tastes disgusting, and her pajamas are scratchy. She cannot understand why she has to stop doing what she wants to do, and she hates going to bed! Being in bed is uncomfortable, she hears her heart beating in the pillow, she feels her pulse, her thoughts are on full blast, and she can hear every movement of every person in the house. Even with just the night-light on, it is too light, but she is terrified of the dark, so closing her eyes is not an option. She re-runs the events of the day in her mind, but never in order and never accurately. Trying to lie still in the bed intensifies the replay of sensory experiences from the day, and she really wants to scream. She starts rocking to make it all go away, and then she hums to make the noise of her own pulse quiet down. She cannot find any of her "off" buttons, so she is stuck in the state of heightened sensitivity, and it takes a long time to fall asleep.

Jamie would benefit from some simple interventions. In school, if the teachers could provide her with a visual of the lesson plan, then any time Jamie loses focus, she can bring her attention back "online" by looking at the lesson plan to re-enter the lesson from the point she left. This is a good strategy for all students with ADHD of any type. This student with inattentive ADHD goes on occasional "attention vacations," so having some kind of guide to use to re-orient upon re-entry is a great help. Jamie would have benefited by a visual chart at home that listed what she had to do, if possible in the order that she had to do it. The need for sameness and predictability is an aspect of the autistic need for precision, so implementing a regular after-school schedule can be very helpful. Regular, predictable, repeatable schedules can be as necessary to the autistic person as oxygen. Although it is not always the most natural or comfortable mode for the family, it can re-establish a sense of safety and security for the autistic person. A regular, consistent schedule for Jamie would mean she could use what little attention energy she had left after the long school day for controlling how her attention gets applied during her homework. She would find the interactions with her mother less confrontational, and her mother would be less likely to react out of exhausted frustration.

Memory

Memory is one of the most personal experiences we have. No two people have the same memory. While this is an obvious statement, we rarely consider what a profound impact memory has on our ability to process our experiences. The personal nature of memory also makes it difficult to truly understand how someone else builds up his or her memories.

The three basic levels of memory are short-term memory, working memory, and long-term memory.

Short-term memories are generally those quick in-and-out memories, and are:

- based on quick exposure, we process the information and determine if it is important

- re-coded and condensed, or shortened, information

- filtered, sifted, and sorted

- assessed for novelty – we pay attention to novel information

- assessed for importance or interest level – what is the perceived meaning?

- discarded as unnecessary (99% of short-term memories are discarded).

Working memory is the foundation of our daily information processing system, and is:

- a memory that we hold on to for various amounts of time through the day

- able to hold onto a capacity of seven items on average

- the ability to combine short- and long-term memory. It makes it possible for us to hold on to the question while we think of an answer, or remember what we read at the beginning of the paragraph when we arrive at the end

- memory on one track at a time. We do not process two trains of thought at the same time, but we quickly alternate from one to the other.

Long-term memory is where we hold our memories over time. How we get our memories into long-term memory (input) is as important as how we get them back out for use (retrieval). In our long-term memory we:

- consolidate our memories (our memory hard-drive)

- file and access information in our limitless storage system

- use various types of memory such as:

  - procedural memory – how to do something implicit, build skills, remember the order or sequence actions

  - declarative memory – how we store and recall spoken and written information; the memory used when memorizing information, facts, poems, etc.

  - episodic memory – how we remember events or what happened

  - semantic memory – how we remember words and their meaning, grammar, math rules, etc.

We know a great deal about how memory works as well as how memories are formed. Memories come through various portals or modalities, and each of us has naturally stronger or weaker memory input portals. The general input modes for memory are:

- visual – taking in information through seeing

- factual – memory for facts

- motor – remember through doing

- auditory – hearing or processing auditory information

- non-motor procedural – remembering procedure, such as the order in long division

- sequential – order of events

- risk – based in causal thinking, remember when something is dangerous.

We have established that the autistic person has a greater sense of precision and sensitivity, so this will certainly play a role in the formation of and ability to retrieve memories. Most often, we use more than one mode of memory at a time, yet we all have a specific comfort zone with a few of these memory modes. If we are flexible enough, we can shift between these memory modes fairly easily. The autistic child may not have the same level of flexibility, so memories formed on only one or two modes of memory can become rigid. I saw a good example of this with an 11-year-old boy when I was working on writing with him. Somewhere along the line, a teacher had told him it is good to start a sentence with a clause, followed by a comma, before writing the main content of the sentence. So he understood that every sentence must begin with a clause. His memory was firm and he was adamant about this. No matter how much we talked about this as one good option among many others for sentence construction, there was no convincing him otherwise. His auditory memory, combined with his procedural/motor memory, were fixed points, and no matter how logical my comments were, his points of memory were fixed and could not be changed. Gradually, over time, he noticed that no one else started every sentence with a clause, and he began to add simple sentences that were different from what he thought he had been taught. He was able to gradually make the change himself. This is a clear example of how one child's memory was formed and not easily changed, despite clear evidence that the memory was flawed. It highlights an interesting experience of the autistic person in that it is possible to become quite fixed and rigid when recalling one's memories. "I am sure I remember it right!"

This is a different experience from not being able to recall an event at all. We know what it is like to have to say, "I don't remember that happening at all." In working with autistic children, I noticed that when they did recall a memory, it was more often as a fixed memory, retrievable in only one form, and not open for discussion.

When helping a child with autism learn or remember, it helps to use sensory-based memory hooks such as visuals, sounds, textures, etc. Packing the memory with sensory information makes it easier to retrieve, making the input and retrieval more consistent. Memories will be formed more easily if the input is consistent with the language preference of the autistic person (see Chapter 3). Since the autistic person relates so well to the environment or architecture of the space, it is a good idea to use this strength as a method of improving memory. Start with what the person does relate to and remember, and gradually add other pieces of information and details. This makes it easier for the autistic person to call up their own, personal memories, and eventually add other details to the mix.

Organization

The usual organizational disasters of a binder exploding with wrinkled papers, homework that never makes it back to the teacher, pencils that are always lost or broken, and planners that have weeks' worth of blank pages are all well known for students with executive function difficulties. Organization is an executive action that comes about when a student gets an overview of the situation at hand, makes a mental image of what is needed, creates a plan for how to arrange the papers, binders, etc., and then maintains this order on a daily basis. Although it could be expected that this is a bigger problem among children and teenagers, I speak with many adults who also struggle with keeping things organized. For students with autism, organization seems to be linked to their internal sense of order and predictability. There is often little flexibility once a sense of order is set, and any changes in that order can develop into full meltdowns. It can seem at first that the autistic child likes things neat and tidy, always puts their papers away, and can be counted on to be organized for nearly everything. What can actually be going on, though, is that the child has a fixed idea of how the room should look, how the binder should be organized, where their belongings should be, and there is no other option for this organization. Again, this speaks to the inherent flexibility that is usually needed for any executive function to work, and flexibility is generally not an inherent strength of the autistic individual. An autistic person is likely looking for predictability and routine. Whether that predictability is neat and tidy, or chaotic and messy, is not the main issue for the autistic child; the main issue is whether or not it matches their internal sense of how things should go.

In Chapter 2 we met Michael who needs everything to be in order. Michael's mother is able to keep the house predictably tidy and organized, but the one day that Michael came home and she had moved furniture around elicited a major meltdown from Michael that lasted several days. It did not make an impression on Michael that his mother had purchased some new furniture, and that she had told him in advance that the furniture in one room was going to be moved so the new furniture could be used. Michael heard about these plans, but was clearly not forming mental images in preparation for the change. He had not internalized the information so he had no explicit ideas about the changes his mother told him about. So, when Michael arrived home from school, saw that two rooms had been changed, his meltdown was immediate and he was inconsolable. For several days after the room-moving incident, he repeatedly asked about changes, if there would be a change that day when he came home from school. Michael experienced the changes as global changes, not specific to a single room on a single day. As a result of the furniture change, he became unsure about what to expect on other days. His sense of secure, predictable outer organization was thrown into a panic and it took him time to settle down into the soothing, predictable routines again. This type of upset over changes could happen at school, too, but the teachers cannot only avoid this completely, they also cannot always trace the panic or upset about change back to the source.

It is necessary to learn to live with changes; change is inherent in all learning. Even though Michael's parents and teachers would often not be able to observe what small change in pattern or routine had set Michael into a meltdown, they had to keep his world in that fine balance between predictable routine and naturally occurring changes. To their credit, they continued to use preview and review daily, which helped Michael learn to form mental images of events. They continued to give him clear descriptions of what to expect, even days in advance. They tried to imagine what might be difficult for him to adjust to in school situations, and spoke with teachers about how they might present a lesson or describe a homework assignment without assuming that Michael could fill in the implicit parts of the assignment – for example, if they wanted Michael to show his math work, they had to say that explicitly, and not assume that he knew that was an expectation.

Organizing the environment for children like Michael is important in order to minimize the number and severity of changing events. Working with the parents of children with autism, I have gone through a list of options for organization and helped them choose the approaches they not only think will help their child, but also the activities they feel are sustainable in family life. Organization of time, or planning, can be very difficult for the child who is not able to make a relationship to time.

An example of an organizational option related to time management and the organization of space is the daily schedule. The day can be organized on a calendar that is visible to all. Depending on the child, this can be written or presented in pictures. Calendars can be hung on the door or wall, or they can be electronic, if that provides easier access for the child. The hourly schedule is one level, and this is what students have to face since their classes change every hour. The chunked schedule might show what is happening in the morning, afternoon, or evening. The full day schedule might show what is happening on a given day, such as a field trip or a visit from a special person. A project calendar shows the overview of the project with set goals from beginning to end. When the executive skills are working well, students are fluidly flexible and able to shift between these examples of daily schedule organization. As discussed in previous sections, flexibility is difficult for the individual with autism, so calendars need to be made visual, concrete, and explicit.

Outer organization is important, so the room can be predictably arranged and organized, clothes can be put in the same place each time, and the number of items in the space can be reduced so the autistic person can get a visual overview. Whether organization is done by or for the autistic person makes a difference. Long-term organizational skills are developed through personal experience, so it is a good idea to start with something that the autistic individual can do alone, and practice that for a time before adding other organizational skills to the mix. Since it is often more effective to start small, choose one small thing, such as the math papers getting filed in the math folder each day. Yes, this does seem like a small item, but it might be manageable, and therefore far more productive than a task that is more difficult or complex, and therefore a task that the student will fail to fulfill. Small successes are meaningful and important, so start small, and be happy for the small successes.

Planning

Just as organization is often related to our physical surroundings, planning is related to our ability to manage time. I ask students some unexpected questions before we actually start working on time management, since their answers will provide essential insights into how they form mental images of time. These are real questions and real answers that I have received over the years from students, with and without autism.

Me: "What month does the year start with?"

Student: "I don't know – May?"

Me: "Let's start with January – what comes next?"

Student: "February, March, May, April, June, July, September, November, December?"

Since this answer is not correct, I know a few things. The sequencing of the information is not in place, the memory hooks for the order of the year aren't activated, and the student is not creating a mental picture for the year. For some reason, October is left off the list most frequently. So we go back over the list, correct it, and get the months in order.

Then I ask about the month. How many days are in a month? The answers I get are as varied as 15 to 40. When a student does know that it is either 30 or 31, we deal with February as the anomaly. We might do the little verse that repeats the days in a month, or show on our knuckles how to count if a month has 30 or 31 days. The difficulty with the knuckle-counting approach is that it requires the student to know the months of the year in order.

How do you picture the days in the week? Most students know how to name the days of the week in order, but few can answer when I ask how they picture the days of the week. They are simply words to be said in order, so it is not possible to picture the weekdays in June as different from the weekdays in September.

The hours of the day offer their own challenges – since most students nowadays have learned to tell time on a digital clock rather than an analog clock, they often do not picture the whole day. I ask students to describe how they picture the hours of a day, and one day a student said he had no picture of time. I was a bit surprised, so I asked if he could picture the hour that just passed. He said no. So I asked how he pictured the hour to come, and he said he has no picture about time that hadn't come yet. I asked him what he did picture, and he answered just the time in the moment.

He went on to explain that just as it is on a digital clock, the only time he sees is the minute that is up, the immediate present, and what went before and what is to come made no impression on him. This student was the first one who described this to me, but he was not the last.

Not only do these students not form pictures of time, their relationship with past, present, and future ranges from weak to non-existent. If we put this together with the previous comments about the importance of review and preview for healthy executive function, then how can a student develop healthy executive skills if they have essentially no working relationship with the past, present, and future?

Developing a relationship to time will be dependent on the student's language preferences, as discussed in Chapter 3, as well as their relationship to the AAPs in Chapter 4, but it is essential to form a mental picture of time in order to eventually manage time independently. I find that creating some basic images of time can help, and I might start by asking if the student knows where the sun comes up in the morning. Then we might talk about the movement of the sun across the sky and an outer manifestation of time passing. If we did not have clocks, how could time be tracked? We can start with sundials and hourglasses, and eventually transfer the movement of the sun onto an analog clock. Visual timers come next, especially the ones that show the movement of time. I do not begin with these timers, though, because they usually have a full circle representing an hour, so 15 minutes will be represented as one quarter of the circle. On an analog clock, we teach that the full circle represents 12 hours. It can take some flexibility for the student to see the quarter of an hour on a timer as different from the equivalent of 3 hours on a clock. It takes explicit practice for a student to bridge the sense of time with the way we actually track time. Show it, move it, draw it, make it practical and imaginative. Above all, make it engaging so that the sense of time can grow from an experience into a concept.

Inhibition and initiative

Few students I work with even know what these words mean, so beginning with a definition is a good idea. It can be as simple as the stop and go button. Initiative is making the decision to start an action, and inhibition is that which makes it possible to stop an action. It sounds simple at first, but it is connected to a state of consciousness that is very individual. Being able to delay gratification is correlated to emotional maturity, so making a decision to stop or start an action is certainly high on the maturity scale. In order to be able to inhibit an action, the individual has to see the consequences of not inhibiting that action.

"If I take my brother's ball without asking, he will get mad at me."

"If I go outside the house without asking, my parents will worry and be upset."

"If I tell the teacher I don't want to do the math test, I will get in trouble and have to do it anyway."

These are big examples, with a clear-cut correlation between cause and effect. Causality of this nature is consciously understood when the student is closer to the age of 12, but earlier than that the non-autistic child has learned any number of consequences and is able to inhibit behavior in relation to those actions. The autistic person might not be able to notice the correlation between cause and effect in the same way. In Michael's example (see Chapter 3), he could not link cause and effect. He was not able to understand what was expected of him because he did not understand that what his mother could see (the time) caused her to identify the effect (it is time to go). All Michael knew was what he saw, so unless the situation was put in terms of what he could see and experience, there would be no reason to either initiate action or inhibit behavior. For Michael, his actions were only initiated in relation to his personal experience of the world around him, not in relation to what was being asked of him by another person.

The same is true for inhibiting behaviors in that Michael was engaged in an action that made sense to him, and being told by someone else to stop made no sense. Inhibition does not easily work when it comes from the outside of the child. Being told to start or stop an action feels like an abuse of power because it is not arising from within the individual's personal experience. This carries on into adulthood and is just as true for the autistic adult. It is much better to create an environment in which the autistic adult can make personal decisions about what to do and how to act rather than impose either initiative or inhibition upon the person from the outside.

Flexibility

It is a well-known phenomenon that autistic individuals can appear stubborn. I am not really sure this is true stubbornness, or if it is simply a lack of flexibility. We have already established that autistic individuals have a hard time adapting to change. The examples abound, in that changes in an autistic person's environment or schedule can elicit profound reactions. The autistic person has a greater degree of precision and sensitivity, which means that they experience change with a greater degree of precision and sensitivity. Change is a natural part of life, though, so the autistic person has to be allowed to find ways to become more flexible in order to cope with the naturally occurring changes that make up everyday life.

Instead of simply imposing changes on an autistic person that they have to accept, first identify the parts of everyday life that will not be changed and that can be relied on to remain consistent. Identify the areas of consistency that are acceptable in the given situation, and focus on making these areas comfortably consistent for a time. Examples include how clothes are folded and where they are kept; the order for a morning routine, such as getting dressed and then eating breakfast; eating at the same table and sitting in the same place at the table; using predictable utensils at breakfast. These examples can go on and on, but it is possible to see that there are many options in the course of a day to identify what can be consistent and repeatable.

Then it is time to add in flexibility. The school schedule is set up on an "A" day and a "B" day, so the schedule is only the same every other day. This can be enormously challenging to some autistic students who crave sameness every day. It is good if that student's flexibility has not been used up in the simple things such as how to get ready for school and what to eat for breakfast. This holds true for autistic adults as well. Life will be full of surprises that require flexibility, but if all the flexibility is used up on areas that could be made predictable, then there is little left over for those challenging situations that call for flexibility.

Flexibility extends beyond the daily schedule and habits. All social interactions require flexibility in that one must listen to what others are saying and respond appropriately, rather than simply following the thoughts in one's own head. Social interaction is active, changing, and dynamic. These three qualities all require high degrees of flexibility, so it may need to be taught to an autistic person. This is a clear example of the importance of Pia's quote at the beginning of the book stating that learning executive function skills is more important than learning social skills.

Control of behavior and emotion

We have already used the definition of executive function as the functions in our brain that control attention and behavior. Linking behavior and emotion is not that far off from this central activity of our executive brain. Behavior and emotion are similar in that they both require a lifetime of learning and practice to master our behavior and our emotions. I would guess that few people feel they have achieved the level of mastery in either of these areas. Our behavior and emotions are learning curves that are in a constant state of change and evolution, so we already know that this kind of growth and self-control is going to be challenging for the autistic person. The behaviors of children are naturally controlled from the outside, by parents and adults who are tasked with the safety and education of the child. Autistic children find this difficult, and adapt slowly to being changed by others.

Throughout this book we have talked about various approaches to creating change by first creating predictability, moving slowly, and involving the autistic person as much as possible in the process. These principles hold true for teaching control of behavior. Identifying the behavior that needs to be changed is the first step, and then recognizing how many behaviors are already in place to support the change is the second step. This is really the core principle in what is referred to as "behavior modification," but I prefer to approach behavior changes through the salutogenic model (see Chapter 2).

1. Identify the behavior and make it comprehensible. When, where, why, and how is the behavior manifesting?

2. Identify why this behavior is relevant and decide if it needs to be changed. Make a meaningful assessment of the behavior, and include the autistic person as much as possible in this process.

3. Establish manageable steps for change. Remember how hard change is for the autistic person, so make it explicit, targeted, and manageable.

This might seem like a long process at first, but it is more successful than going after change purely from a perspective of reward and punishment. While some behavior change models do include specific rewards and punishments, it cannot be the only option used to bring about behavior changes for autistic individuals. Successful behavior changes take time, and are a necessary part of human growth and development. Autistic and non-autistic individuals alike need help with behavior changes at times, and a great deal of patience is required when engaging an autistic person in a change process.

Emotional control is not that different from behavioral control in that both benefit from the salutogenic approach. It is a little more complicated with emotional control because it can only be brought into the change process once it manifests as an emotion. The gentle and controlled emotions are not noticed so much, but the hot and messy emotions are easy for all to see. The same holds true for emotional outbursts as well as behavior outbursts. It is crucial to try to identify the source of the disturbance, and work from there. The example of the girl who melted down, crying and yelling "No lasagna!!" is such an example. Her emotions and behavior could not be changed in that instant without removing the source of the reaction. Once she was clear that she was not going to be forced to eat the lasagna, she could be guided toward a different emotion and behavior. Simply telling her to calm down and stop yelling and crying would have been useless. The salutogenic approach for the girl could include telling her in a quiet moment that you understand she does not like lasagna, and that in the future you will have alternative food ready for her. Then, on the next day that lasagna is served, tell her as early in the day as you can, and give her a sensory experience of the food you will give her instead. This will make her behavior and emotion more comprehensible, meaningful, and manageable, and therefore more controllable.

Goal setting

Executive functions rely heavily on the individual being able to set goals all the time, consciously and unconsciously. We are possibly more familiar with conscious goal setting because we could not get through the average day without them. Our goal setting starts as soon as we wake up, and we become aware of what we need to do that day, and in what order it needs to be done. Parents are fully immersed in goal setting before their feet hit the floor, and the steady stream of decisions, actions, and goals that will fill their day begins early. Wake the children, make breakfast, get them ready for school, remember all the bits and pieces of the day and be aware of what is needed for each part of the day – gym clothes, musical instruments, sports gear, etc. The non-parent adult has no fewer goals and decisions to make; they are just related to a different area of life and work. The student will be thinking ahead to the day, mentally counting off if everything is ready and if all papers and homework are where they should be. Sounds nice, doesn't it? When the executive brain is processing goals in relation to daily activities, it is also busily engaged in a constant stream of preview and review. What is coming up today? Did I do what was needed to be ready? Where have I put the things I need? Who else in the family needs help to get ready? Review and preview are on full blast.

But the autistic person is not necessarily engaged in this process. They might feel cold getting out of bed in the morning, so until this is managed and stopped, nothing else is important. Then the process of getting dressed triggers reactions because, even though he or she helped set the clothes out the night before, this morning they are the wrong color or they look scratchy. Again, until this is managed, no other goal for behavior is possible. The next obstacle comes at the breakfast table where almost everything looks normal, except the apples are green rather than red, and that is disturbing. A meltdown begins to bubble and form, but someone notices quickly enough and simply removes the apples. This time, it works. It won't work every time, but it does work this time. It is time to go to school and everyone in the family has set and met literally hundreds of goals, but the autistic member of the family is working slowly from one potential crisis to the other.

Explicitly teaching a student about goals can be done by the same approach as with control of behavior and emotion:

1. Set a goal that is comprehensible.

2. Make sure the goal is relevant.

3. Identify ways to make the goal manageable.

This is achieved by following all the previously mentioned principles: start small, make changes slowly, and involve the autistic person in every step of the process. Change is hard, and the autistic person deserves respect and understanding for their experiences.

6

The Executive Function Map

Making the Kaleidoscope Coherent

Key points

- The Executive Function Map offers a way of organizing and understanding the individual applications of the eight executive skills in daily life.

- Four questions help reveal how the autistic individual uses his or her executive functions:

  - Strengths/weaknesses: what are your competencies? What do you find difficult?

  - Learning goals: what is your agenda? What are your intentions?

  - Accommodations: how should your approach be structured? What support should be provided?

  - Strategies: what strategies will be used to realize your learning goals?

- The completed Executive Function Map can be used by the individual as a tool for self-reflection, or by teachers or parents as a tool for identifying learning needs, and creating learning goals and accommodations to support learning outcomes.

• Perhaps the most important executive function is the ability to review and preview. If this can be taught first, followed by the other executive functions, then learning social skills falls into a context that make more sense.

The kaleidoscope returns in a supporting role when we create an Executive Function Map. Most of the time, we look at single executive skills and focus on the effect in daily life. Through making an Executive Function Map, we bring all the skills together and start to form a picture of their interrelationships, and we start seeing the isolated parts of the kaleidoscope in one view.

In my previous book (Moraine 2012), the Executive Function Map was built on the following questions:

• What are your strengths in this area?

• What are your weaknesses in this area?

• What goals do you have in this area?

• What strategies are you going to use to meet these goals?

These questions provide a self-reflective tool for the individual to begin thinking about his or her own executive skills in an objective context. If the individual cannot write this map alone or independently, then someone else can guide this process. I have created Executive Function Maps with individuals and with groups, and in every instance the answers have been very individualized as well as insightful.

When filling out an Executive Function Map with an autistic individual, the questions can be asked a bit more explicitly. If the capacity of the autistic individual allows him or her to engage with these questions independently, then the map can be used in a similar manner, namely, as a tool for self-reflection and self-knowledge. If the student is not able to engage at that level, then this map becomes a very handy tool for identifying learning needs through observation and direct experience of the autistic student. The insights gained from the map can then be translated into learning goals, outcomes and accommodations to support those learning outcomes. In this situation, the map may need to be filled out by the parent or teacher, since the student may not be able to articulate the answers clearly enough to identify learning strategies. The questions focus on strengths and weaknesses, learning goals, accommodations needed, and approaches to making the accommodations effective.

1. Strengths/weaknesses: what are your competencies? What do you find difficult?

2. Learning goals: what is your agenda? What are your intentions?

3. Accommodations: how should your approach be structured? What support should be provided?

4. Strategies: what strategies will be used to realize your learning goals?

In the following pages are examples of Executive Function Maps for students in middle school and high school who have autism and ADHD. The information in an Executive Function Map can be used at home and with friends, or as the basis of an IEP for executive function at school. However this map is used, whether in fine detail or in a generalized way, it can shed light on the strengths/weaknesses of the individual, and the specific approaches needed to improve his or her executive skills in daily life.

Table 5.1: Attention

Attention	**Strengths**	I am good at paying attention to one thing at a time.
	Weaknesses	I can't pay attention to someone talking and write at the same time (classroom demands, taking notes, etc.).
	Learning goals	Learn how to shift between listening and writing.
	Accommodations	Provide an outline of notes for class to lessen the demand for note-taking.
	Approaches	Lessen the amount of attention shifts needed between listening and writing simultaneously by giving an outline of the notes.
Attention	**Strengths**	I am good at paying attention to what interests me.
	Weaknesses	I don't pay attention to anything that does not interest me.
	Learning goals	Expand areas of interest to make learning more meaningful.
	Accommodations	Begin with areas of interest when introducing new material.
	Approaches	Use review and preview by starting with an area of interest in the review and introducing the new area of learning in the preview.
Attention	**Strengths**	I make attention decisions that suit my structures.
	Weaknesses	I can get stuck and not be able to start a new attention decision if I don't get to choose how to set my attention myself.
	Learning goals	Use own attention decisions and keep them short enough to keep attention on track by using new decisions frequently.
	Accommodations	Provide movement opportunities, sensory items, and various focal points.
	Approaches	Let me choose when to stand up, move around, have different places to work, and re-set my brain with each new attention decision.

Table 5.2: Memory

Memory	**Strengths**	I remember everything I read.
	Weaknesses	I don't remember what people say to me.
	Learning goals	Use visual cues as often as possible to support verbal instructions.
	Accommodations	Repeat verbal instructions when visual cues are not available.
	Approaches	Use visuals and present instructions in a written format as often as possible.
Memory	**Strengths**	I have good tactile memory.
	Weaknesses	I have a hard time remembering what people show me when I can't touch it.
	Learning goals	Do it to learn it.
	Accommodations	Let me try to touch it and engage with what I am learning.
	Approaches	Don't rely only on books or concepts, but let me build it, touch it, and interact with it. Let me learn to play a musical instrument rather than learn about music theory.
Memory	**Strengths**	I remember what I hear.
	Weaknesses	I can't stand it when too much is going on and I can't focus on what I am hearing.
	Learning goals	Find a way to use hearing as a strength in learning.
	Accommodations	Use text to speech software if reading is difficult; record information and directions; provide auditory access to information when possible.
	Approaches	Ask for the directions to be spoken, and ask for repeats of directions or information whenever needed.

Table 5.3: Organization

Organization	Strengths	I can keep my papers well organized.
	Weaknesses	It is hard for me to keep my thoughts organized.
	Learning goals	Keep track of thoughts so the work can be done.
	Accommodations	Have an outline, graphic organizer, or list of topics to cover provided in writing.
	Approaches	Write down my plans, record my ideas so I have a paper copy to keep track of my work.
Organization	Strengths	I like to have a clean space so I can keep everything tidy.
	Weaknesses	Once things get untidy it is hard for me to organize them again.
	Learning goals	Keep working space tidy and organized.
	Accommodations	Provide a work area that is prepared in advance and organized for the specific work that needs to be done.
	Approaches	Agree on the initial organization and re-organize as frequently as needed to maintain an optimal amount of organization. Let me set up my space the way I want it so I can make it tidy the way it works for me.
Organization	Strengths	I like things functional and predictable.
	Weaknesses	It is upsetting when anything is changed in my space.
	Learning goals	To be able to adapt to changes with minimal warning or preparation.
	Accommodations	Give a verbal or written warning about upcoming changes.
	Approaches	Ask for information in advance of changes in both the room (environment) and expectations (assignments and work).

Table 5.4: Planning

Planning	Strengths	I have a good sense of rhythm.
	Weaknesses	I get very upset if events occur out of rhythm.
	Learning goals	Set plans in place even if they are out of rhythm.
	Accommodations	Set up long-term and short-term planning calendars.
	Approaches	Have access to the long-term and short-term planning, and show the changes made to either calendar. Hear in advance of changes – preview any change in rhythm, and review changes to be sure they were done.
Planning	Strengths	I plan based on predicting what is coming up.
	Weaknesses	I can't adjust to a change in my plans that I didn't see coming.
	Learning goals	To remain engaged in the plan even if a change happened. Create a new calendar with the change included.
	Accommodations	Communicate all changes to plans and calendar quickly and effectively.
	Approaches	Maintain an online calendar that can be automatically updated when change occurs.
Planning	Strengths	I plan when the event is recurring, using visuals.
	Weaknesses	I have to write down my plan for how I am going to handle an event, or I have to ask someone for help since I don't like social interactions and can't join a social interaction without a plan for my involvement.
	Learning goals	Learn how to write things down on an "internal blackboard" and retrieve plans from other sources.
	Accommodations	Have access to writing down everything I have to plan. Have access to school plans in writing (online, class websites, etc.). Maintain a calendar on the wall as well as an electronic calendar.
	Approaches	Always have a notebook or electronic device that I can write things down so I don't forget.

Table 5.5: Inhibition and initiative

Inhibition and initiative	**Strengths**	I am good at starting things if I understand what I am supposed to do.
	Weaknesses	I don't like to stop when I am doing what I want to do.
	Learning goals	To recognize when it is a good time to start doing what I want to do.
	Accommodations	Provide clear guidelines to communicate when an activity is allowed.
	Approaches	Set up in advance so it is clear that specific situations allow for specific behavior. For example, in reading class it is permissible to read about salamanders, but it is not allowed during math class.
Inhibition and initiative	**Strengths**	I am good at asking questions and steering the conversation toward what I understand.
	Weaknesses	I am not good at following someone else's initiative.
	Learning goals	Learn how to ask questions differently or follow the initiative of someone else, even if I don't understand it at first.
	Accommodations	Share the initiative in more than one format (verbal, auditory, visual, tactile).
	Approaches	Let me take the initiative and ask my question first, then, if it has to be changed, let me re-formulate my question so I can stay engaged in the process.
Inhibition and initiative	**Strengths**	I know when I am in a social situation I have to be careful what I say.
	Weaknesses	It is hard for me to say the right thing in social situations.
	Learning goals	To learn how to initiate a social conversation, ask for help in school, or read social cues for engaging in a social conversation.
	Accommodations	Lead into the conversation by letting me know when it is a good time for me to ask my question or by giving me a cue that it is a good time to engage in a social exchange.
	Approaches	Use conversation starters to give me an idea about what is appropriate to talk about; use verbal and visual cues if I go off-track in a conversation.

Table 5.6: Flexibility

Flexibility	**Strengths**	I can be flexible once I understand what is being asked of me.
	Weaknesses	I often don't understand what is being asked of me.
	Learning goals	To become more responsive to what is being asked, to be able to change my course of action even if I don't want to.
	Accommodations	Keep the request for change specific to a single situation.
	Approaches	When I have to be flexible, find more than one way to communicate this and give me a clear description of what I need to do. Don't assume I know what you mean if you don't say it clearly.
Flexibility	**Strengths**	I can respond to requests to change.
	Weaknesses	I cannot change too many things at once.
	Learning goals	To respond flexibly to change – especially when the change request comes from a person in authority.
	Accommodations	Give reasons for requests to change and put the request in more than one format.
	Approaches	Describe what is going to change in understandable images, and give time for me to respond or adjust.
Flexibility	**Strengths**	I respect structure.
	Weaknesses	I can get overwhelmed in situations with little structure – I not only respect structure, but I cannot do without it.
	Learning goals	To adapt to situations with less structure, or establish structure where needed.
	Accommodations	Provide predictable structure to assignments and engagement in any activity.
	Approaches	Give individual choices for engaging in a project or assignment, but don't give too many choices. Once a structure is in place, don't change it quickly or often.

Table 5.7: Control of behavior and emotion

Control of behavior and emotion	Strengths	I am good at not blurting out in a social situation.
	Weaknesses	I often don't know what is appropriate to say and do.
	Learning goals	To get better at knowing what I can say or do in a social situation.
	Accommodations	Give clear and consistent guidance or feedback about social interactions.
	Approaches	Help me set up clear behaviors of social interaction before the event; help me picture a social interaction and practice effective behaviors for the situation.
Control of behavior and emotion	Strengths	I spend time alone.
	Weaknesses	I don't like social interactions, and it is hard for me to engage with people I don't know. It makes me nervous to talk with people, especially new people.
	Learning goals	Be comfortable enough with other people so I can look them in the eye and greet them.
	Accommodations	Keep social interactions to a minimum; introduce new people and social demands one at a time.
	Approaches	Introduce me to someone, then give me time to adjust so that person can become a familiar person to me rather than simply a new person.
Control of behavior and emotion	Strengths	I am a hard worker and always try to get my work done and I try to do and say the right thing when interacting with other people.
	Weaknesses	If I get overwhelmed, I melt down – I cry, yell, scream, run away, whatever it takes to make it stop.
	Learning goals	To keep the work and social demands at a reasonable level.
	Accommodations	Assign the work or activity and don't change it before I am finished. If a meltdown is imminent or already happened, give me some time and space to recover before asking me to review it.
	Approaches	Give warnings in the form of previewed review previous behavior frequently.

Table 5.8: Goal setting

Goals	**Strengths**	I am good at knowing what I want to do.
	Weaknesses	I have a hard time if what I need to do is not what I want to do.
	Learning goals	To set up my learning goals in advance so I have time to adjust to goals I don't like.
	Accommodations	Give course syllabus and assignments in advance; post assignment deadlines and quizzes in advance; post expectations in a retrievable place.
	Approaches	Use review and preview every day so I am prepared for what is coming, and make it easier to do what I don't like doing.
Goals	**Strengths**	I am good at setting blocks of activity.
	Weaknesses	I can sometimes get so engaged in what I am doing that I don't know when or how to stop.
	Learning goals	To let my stop and start times be determined by someone else.
	Accommodations	Set start and stop times in advance, and provide a visual clock/timer to follow the time.
	Approaches	Set up the full activity in advance, preview what is going to happen, decide on an effective amount of time needed for the activity.
Goals	**Strengths**	I set up my activity from parts to the whole.
	Weaknesses	I can't see the whole before I see the smaller parts that lead to it.
	Learning goals	Be able to see what the whole project entails.
	Accommodations	Set out guidelines, expectations, and approaches in advance. Create a mental picture, then work from that picture to identify the details.
	Approaches	Get all my information together first, set out the various parts, and then start working on putting it all together. This is especially important in writing where I need to have lots of ideas and parts before I can weave them into a whole.

To repeat, one of the most essential executive skills is the ability to preview and review. This cannot be stressed enough. Through reflection we look back on previous experiences and recall how the previous experience played out, and what we found worked well and what did not work well. With that information we assess our current or present situation, and decide if we are going to do the same as last time or do something different. Then we plan our new activity. This takes many words to express, but in fact, this happens in less time than we can imagine. The only reason we need to slow this down enough to wrap words around it is so we can understand why the activity of review and preview are so vital to the development of effective executive function in everyday life. The ability to make a decision in the moment based on previous experiences is the fundamental principle of executive function as well as education. Nearly every pedagogical engagement is based on this one basic activity. We learn to read and comprehend what we read based on this principle. The laws of math and science are learned based on this principle. Our ability to interact with others is based on this principle. For the autistic person, this is easier in relation to academic learning because facts do not change from one day to the other. Facts can be learned and added to other facts, and this can go on without ever changing in that law of truth. Interactions with other people are more difficult because they can change with every encounter, so the law of what to do or say in a social encounter is harder to learn. This is one reason why it is so much easier for the autistic person to excel at academic learning and still be quite uncomfortable in a social situation.

Social skills are also important, but if the activity of review and preview as the fundamental aspect of executive function can be taught first, followed by the other executive functions, then learning social skills falls into a context that make more sense. The executive functions then bring order into the chaos, and are especially needed for the autistic experience. The Executive Function Map helps the autistic person comprehend their experiences, find meaning or relevance in their experiences, and identify the tools that will make those experiences manageable. This brings the individual's engagement with executive skills full circle back to the original idea of salutogenesis, or a sense of coherence.

Conclusion

The quote from Pia at the beginning of this book holds especially true after everything we have learned about executive function.

> I think that teaching executive function to people with autism
> is even more important than teaching social skills.

In our "normal" interaction, we challenge the autistic person to relate to our social structures, to learn in environments that we have set up for non-autistic individuals, and to navigate a world of action that is based on non-autistic norms for behavior. This book offers a "reverse translation" by translating the autistic experience first, and asking the non-autistic individual to make a relationship with the autistic experience before asking the autistic person to relate to the non-autistic world. As a rule of thumb, teachers/coaches, therapists, and parents are only able to guide the development of the executive skills that have first been individually developed. For non-autistic individuals, attention, memory, organization, planning, inhibition and initiative, flexibility, control of behavior and emotions, and the ability to set goals are all executive challenges that need to be understood and be under a reasonable amount of personal control. The more mature the executive skills are, the more the non-autistic person will be able to engage in reverse translation.

When speaking a language, there might be a limited number of words available, but there are unlimited options for putting these words together to form communication. This means that our opportunities to translate will never end. No matter how well we think we understand the autistic person, there will always be more to translate, more to understand, and more to learn about the autistic experience. Relationships between autistic and non-autistic individuals contain limitless possibilities for communication, relationship, and growth. Using the pathway of executive functions can make these relationships richer and more meaningful, so the gift of translation is one that keeps on giving.

Appendix: Pia Hämäläinen's personal description of her experience as an autistic adult

This book is primarily about the child's experience of autism and the slowly maturing executive functions. However, every child with autism eventually becomes an adult with autism. This book came about due to the remarkable conversation between Pia and myself, so it is fitting to include Pia's personal experience of autism directly through excerpts from our correspondence.

> *Thank you for having written this wonderful book (*Helping Students Take Control of Everyday Executive Functions – The Attention Fix*). I myself am autistic (HFA, highly functioning autistic), and as I read the book I am constantly learning new ways to manage executive functions myself. I structure my life by always structuring my attention first. In my view, the autistic universe is produced by scheduling an "action situation," whereas the non-autistic world is created by scheduling "social situations." Executive function (EF) skills can then be applied to action situation as far as autistics are concerned, and to social situation as far as non-autistics are concerned. I love the very humane, understanding, and respectful way you depict teaching the ingredients and the executive functions.*
>
> *It is great that you include adults. Many times, adults with EF issues have no one to help them. For example, I use rhythm for my days, and I structure my activities around a*

predictable rhythm. Many people use routine with autistic people, but the more suitable solution would be to use rhythm. Let me take the initiative here and tell you more about my story.

I spent years in a care facility for severely autistic individuals because I needed this environment. It was highly structured and interactions were based on activities rather than social interactions. I noticed many autistic people have trouble with interactions at least in part due to the constitution of autistic subjectivity. Autistic subjectivity is a state of flow based on the logic "something is done by an agent." Autistic focus on the activity within a structure and subjectivity is manifested in an objective form through choices and goals. The neurotypical logic "someone does something" puts emphasis on who is doing what, and the autistic logic "something is done by an agent" puts emphasis on the activity itself. Due to this different emphasis on activity, autistic people have difficulty with dividing attention. Autistic people need to be assigned functional roles in action situations (such as taking pictures at a party, so they don't have to talk with anyone) instead of social roles. This affects attention decisions and the way one takes initiative. I love communicating through the passive voice, for example, "The cat is taken care of."

My question was, "Is autism a structural problem, rather than a mental problem?" I applied Louis Althusser's term "interpellation into discourse"[1] here, where individuals are interpolated into existing ideology and become tied to it. With autistic subjectivity, I feel the ideology needs to change. My assumption is that autism is not an illness or a disorder, but an ontological phenomenon that needs to be understood and met with suitable cultural insight. I am an autism theorist, but these thoughts come out of my experiences.

---

1   See https://faculty.washington.edu/mlg/courses/definitions/Interpellation.html

Autistic subjectivity is like a sports team where every member follows the team strategy and plays each situation in such a way that grants victory to the team. This means that each player functions through his or her strengths.

I go into each social situation with my own "game plan," which is "be a blessing in words and deeds in functional roles." My priorities are my cat, my work, my music, God, and a few hand-picked one-to-one relationships. People who visit me know my structure, and I understand them through their structure. I see people as living in parallel worlds, and I can relate to other people through analogies, such as "my love for my cat in my system corresponds to John's love for his kids." I need these actions within structure so I can remain objective and not withdraw from contact. I know my words are a bit idiosyncratic due to my autism, and to the fact that English is not my native tongue, but I do most of my theoretical thinking in English.

A priority that connects me to society at large is culture. TV formats provide predictability and structure, and I love going to concerts, opera, theatre, and art exhibits. I like knowing how to behave in these predictable situations.

It is sometimes difficult to know what autistic people want because they lack experiences and ways to communicate. In such cases, it is important to offer possibilities for experiences. If communication skills are lacking, it is important to read reactions and behavior (like I do with my cat), and based on these observations, draw conclusions. It can be hard for an autistic person to fix attention on too many things, so I choose one or two things to pay attention to.

I find that autistic people, like myself, get lost in processes without goal-orientation. That is why autistic people become easily ritualistic. This is very dysfunctional, and offering goals makes us more functional. I need daily structures and goals to get dressed, eat breakfast, feed the cat, etc. The autistic person is always in a state of process, but these goals channel process in productive ways. Autistic individuals do things and are thus "agents," and only feel like themselves in a process with goals. Goals give me a sense of myself.

Autistic subjectivity and goal-oriented agency are concerned with whole to the parts and parts to the whole. Parts to the whole is relevant when learning who one is. One needs to try on many small ideas, see what happens, and keep what works. The whole to the parts approach establishes a defined structure such as a daily, weekly, monthly schedule. One needs to set clearly defined goals to focus on and define the steps to achieve these goals.

[The conversation switched to sensory questions.] At the Autism Foundation, they try to reduce sensory data by using portioned walls, thus creating some sort of isolation from sensory data. I find this helps me focus on my work. I use earplugs when I can. The problem for students at school is that they cannot block out the teacher with walls and earplugs. But I find sensory data less disturbing when I know what to focus on, or if I have focal points. This gives me a more active role in processing sensory data. I think it is important to use one's preferred sensory channel, and train one's senses. Some call this "sensory de-sensitization."

It is important to let students learn at their own pace, and not to introduce too many items at once. I find it important to take a break before a paradigm shift. Your "attention decisions" are also important here, and I have used them to find my natural pace. It is important not to impose a normative pace on an autistic person. I also find it important to have a lot of personal space physically and mentally. I avoid social touch, I need time to find my pace (more than you would expect), and I don't like force in my interactions. We need to respect that people on the spectrum have difficulties, and we need to accept that.

When you write, sometimes I think you want to help autistic people adjust to normalcy, but my emphasis is to relate to normalcy. Adjusting is one-sided, but relating to normalcy allows for individual solutions. I am rigid socially so the cost is too high to try to "become normal," but I can relate to it. I can observe reactions and behaviors, but I don't see what people's intentions are. I have heard that Baron-Cohen (1997) refers to this as "autistic mindblindness."

I use the ingredients from your book every day, now. I need to trust my relationships, know that analytical skills and my life experiences are my strengths, and my limited interactions and social abilities are my weaknesses. I work from parts to the whole, and I need rhythm to get things done. Once I know the rhythm, I can use routine to continue to practice the skill. EF and the ingredients make my life less uncertain.

I think people with autism should be taught behaviors explicitly. Behavior defines reality: reaction, interaction, communication, EF, thinking, feeling, action, socially appropriate behavior that respects others.

I have been thinking about attention deficit hyperactivity disorder (ADHD) and autism in relation to EF. People with autism seem to depend too much on structure whereas people with ADHD seem to depend too little on structure. Either way, it is important to understand the structure of EF and use it. I see many people with a dual diagnosis of ADHD and autism. That means we would have to know when to teach more structure and when to make do with less structure. My explanation of why your book on EF works so well for people with ADHD and for people with autism is that people with ADHD have social thinking and maybe need help only with EF and people with autism are happy not be taught too much social thinking, but only EF as it applies to activities and social interaction. If you read the criteria about ADHD and autism, they are very similar. If we go with the hypothesis that the big difference is social thinking, and we see both ADHD and autism as ontological phenomena, then it is possible to say they are both good in themselves. Both are centered round creativity related to ideas, but also to social thinking. I have friends with ADHD who relate to the world through empathy, but I relate to the world through intellect; I rely on logic. I feel much less sensitive when I have an intellect-based strategy to relate to sensory stimuli and when I use my senses I prefer vision and hearing. Having the option to talk with you about these things makes me more social. It is a positive social challenge!

You talk about changing only one thing at a time, but that is not always a luxury the autistic person has. Each situation needs a different paradigm, so this is one reason managing change is so difficult for autistic people. The whole configuration changes as situations change. Changing one thing at a time is a luxury autistic adults cannot always afford, because we might be involved in more than one paradigm at a time. Because we work from paradigms, we can learn a skill in one situation, and then that skill disappears when the paradigm shifts. It affects how autistic people learn, so here are some thoughts about autistic learning.

Contact isn't self-evident for people with autism. Contact needs to be established first through interaction – with people, animals, objects, ideas, activities, etc. Many times this crucial phase is skipped and people with autism feel isolated, stuck, and out of touch.

People with autism also have a tendency to focus on aspects. An example of this is when an autistic child focuses on spinning the wheels of a toy car. It is really important to let an autistic person explore aspects: sensory aspects, aspects of an idea, aspects of people, etc. Then we get to construct systems or paradigms for different things, people, and ideas. One problem is that people with autism see the intrinsic value of things, people, ideas, etc. Non-autistic people usually see the social or the use value of things, people, ideas, etc. These are different paradigms. Autistic people need structures for different contexts for their paradigms. Autistic people need strategies and approaches for different situations.

So, yes, the autistic person does what other people do, but in a different order. The autistic person gets to the social through structure, and the non-autistic person gets to structure through being social. Autistic ways of being social are turn-taking instead of reciprocity; giving more time and space for behavior and communication; and pacing interaction to suit the autistic person.

As an autistic person I cannot just respond instinctively to a situation. I have to carefully construct my relationships using the autistic learning method. I have to be explicitly aware of what is going on. I even have to construct and maintain a relationship with myself, and this caused a lot of pain for me before I got the diagnosis of autism. No one, myself included, really understood why it was so hard for me to adjust to situations.

Having autism affects my need for physical space. I need space for behavior and my personal space needs to be bigger. I need to have time alone. I understand when other autistic people care about me and want to smell my hair as a way of showing me their affection, but I cannot bear that.

Most of the time I live in timelessness, in the present. Only deadlines or meetings make me aware of time. I prefer space to time.

I think autistic people need to be tamed like horses, not by breaking them but by being an "Autism Whisperer." Many times autistic people are broken and this causes mental problems. An "Autism Whisperer" is a person who can give structure and order without taking away the person's own will. Young children need structure and order, too, but not in an overbearing or hurtful way. I believe that autism is pretty much a cognitive style and not a disorder in its essence, so we don't have to be broken; we just need to be handled with respect and offered structures. Our personalities are not disorganized, but we do need the proper help to develop. Autism is an earthly condition; it is not a part of our permanent spiritual nature. I feel I know this instinctively.

One thing I struggle with is panic and anxiety. I can wake up in the morning feeling panicky and hysterical. I have to work hard to keep these emotions under control. Many people with autism feel anxious and panicked. This stops my momentum, makes me start procrastinating, and I have to reset the structure of my goals in order to get back on track. Before I learned how to do this for myself, my mom did a lot for me. It made it possible to avoid hysterical outbursts, but it was a bit like learned helplessness or being dysfunctionally functional. I had to learn independence slowly and carefully in order to move away from co-dependent relationships with my family. I just needed more structure in order to achieve this. I needed to be part of a team, with a clear role, and not just have a group membership.

Part of what I struggle with is how to characterize my autism. I am a deep, severe autistic because I need lots of structure and am set in my ways. I have high-functioning autism because I understand normalcy and can live independently with some support. I have Asperger's because I have special interests like cats and my music, learning and cognition. I am a savant because I can chart phenomena and come up with concepts and definitions for phenomena. I can also relate to middle-functioning autistic people who can do normal things but need care 24/7. So, I guess I'm not a normal autistic person but an autistic person who gets many levels of autism. My preference is the company of deeply autistic individuals and their caregivers. I think this is due to my savant abilities – they make me deeply autistic.

One important issue autistic people face is the issue of power vs. empowerment. I always want to start with empowerment by being respectful and understanding. Conceptual thinking helps me here because it gives structure to my interactions. But too much of this is also not good. Conceptual thinking does give me flexibility, though. What really helps me here is autistic subjectivity, which, in general, is about identity, inclinations, gifts, strengths and weaknesses, one's idiosyncratic view of the world, one's ontology, and one's potential to be actualize. Autistic subjectivity empowers me.

Communication is another area that non-autistic people often don't understand. I need to be given yes/no questions. This prevents manipulation and forcing the autistic person to continue some line of reasoning. I need to be offered alternatives to choose from. This addresses the difficulty with taking initiative, since it is easier to choose from alternatives than to come up with the alternatives myself. Saying the same thing in many ways. This is important for me to practice since there are many words that can mean the same thing, so I try to define things unequivocally and ontologically. People might have to repeat the same thing at different times and in different situations in order to get through to me. I like discussing things based on themes – sports, gardening, the weather, etc. I had to learn to ask specific questions in order to continue a conversation.

"How was your vacation?"

"Wonderful!"

Now the conversation could either end or I have to come up with a specific question to ask to get it going again. I had to learn this slowly, and over time. Small talk does not come easily to me. I can easily get caught in what Peter Vermeulen (2011) describes as "context blindness." I can't see what is going on around the event, I can only see the event I am currently engaged in, so asking questions that require me to imagine what someone did on their vacation is very hard, or even impossible. I give feedback based on concepts, but conversations require that one gives feedback based on empathy. What I say might be unwelcome by others because I *might speak it conceptually and objectively, while they might want simply empathy. I am not easily social because of this. I can learn how to be social, though, through understanding EF. This has been a new discovery for me.*

The amount of interaction a severely autistic person needs might be surprising. The need to be managed almost all of the time. For them, interaction is not only with people, but also with objects, surroundings, and ideas. If their senses are acute, then light interaction is called for, but if they are hyposensitive, then more pressure might be needed. The appropriateness of the interaction greatly affects one's willingness to interact in the first place. Interaction is what makes us learn and widen our horizons. I think autistic people can be both hyposocial as well as hypersocial. When I need to be alone, I need to be really alone. I am hyposocial. When I am earnestly interacting with someone, my need for precision can make me hypersocial and it can make others uncomfortable.

In general, I think that the sense of control is a big issue with regards to autism. A sense of one's own subjectivity, and the understanding of one's own agenda, as well as relating to other people's agendas brings a sense of active control. This should always be the goal. Otherwise autistic people are at the mercy of uncoordinated sensory perceptions and other people's agendas they do not discern or understand. Frustration is a common feeling for autistic people. This arises because of communication problems, learning difficulties, not being able to manage a process, control issues, etc. Then we get upset and exhibit challenging behavior such as aggressiveness, meltdowns, hysterics, withdrawal, etc. This is something all autistic people share, and is what gives us our "autism-ness." This is also what makes it hard to find shared experiences between autistic and non-autistic people.

Autistic people start out as autistic children, but we spend most of our lives as adults. While the experiences we have set the tone for our adulthood, I think all ages of experience and learning are meaningful and important.

Glossary

Autism-ness: the essence of the individual autistic experience. It is made up of the individual learning style of the autistic person, the personal manner of processing sensory experiences, the explicit needs of the autistic individual, and the way the autistic individual approaches the world through their personal "autism-nesses."

Autistic Access Points (AAPs): tools for understanding and using executive function. Since the ultimate goal of executive function is to achieve a state of integration or coherence, it is important to gain access to these functions via: relationships; strengths and weaknesses; self-advocacy; review/preview and mental image; whole to the parts and parts to the whole; motivation and incentive; rhythm and routine; implicit and explicit.

Autistic languages: specific ways of communicating that can be used by the autistic individual. Smoothly moving from one language to another may be difficult for the autistic person, so if the autistic individual is engaged in one language (explaining things in conceptual language) it may be very difficult for that person to shift into another language (e.g. emotional language). This is another example where coordination works better than integration, since speaking more than one language at a time can be challenging for the autistic individual. The flexibility afforded to us through our executive function increases our ability to shift more easily between languages.

Emotional language focuses on how we feel – happy, sad, frustrated, enthusiastic, etc. It allows us to express how our actions make us feel. Pragmatic language is the language of both social and practical interactions. It allows us to adjust the way we speak in different situations. Visual language helps us form mental images, which in turns improves our comprehension of the situation. Conceptual language makes it possible to explain things using words and concepts rather than pictures. Kinesthetic language is the language of movement and touch. Social language is the foundation of our interactions with others. Sensory language includes all our senses.

Autistic objectivity and subjectivity: autistic objectivity makes it possible for the autistic person to discern the features and principles of the other, i.e., the "cat-ness" of the cat. This is another form of relating to another object or person rather than adjusting to that object or person. Autistic subjectivity is a term that identifies the subjective, personal, internal experience of autism for the autistic individual. While every person has his or her own subjective experience of the world, the autistic experience is subject to greater degrees of precision and sensitivity, and therefore becomes highly individual and subjective for each person. Exercising both autistic objectivity and autistic subjectivity means the autistic person does not change him or herself in relation to the other person, object, or experience, but rather simply accepts the person, object, or experience at face value. This allows the autistic experience to remain unengaged and is what makes autistic individuals seem like they are "in their own world" so much of the time.

Autistic subjectivity makes it possible for the autistic person to relate to the non-autistic world, since autistic individuals do not find it easy to adjust to the non-autistic world. Keeping these experiences objective makes them easier to understand and process. Adjusting to these non-autistic experiences is very difficult, so the autistic individual will simply relate to them objectively or avoid them altogether.

Executive functions: a set of mental processes that helps connect past experience with present action. These functions help coordinate or integrate what we think, how we feel, and what we do, and there are eight main functions: attention; memory; organization; planning; inhibition and initiative; flexibility; control of behavior and emotion; and goal setting.

The autistic experience of executive functions can be understood through:

- Strengths or competencies – what are an autistic individual's natural strengths?

- Agenda or intentions – what are motivators for the autistic individual?

- Structure – how does the autistic individual relate to the structures presented by the environment?

- Agents – how does the autistic person access action or realize intentions? How do they make a decision to get it done?

Salutogenesis: based on the principle of integration or coherence, made up of these three experiences:

- Comprehensibility – we need to understand what is happening.

- Meaningful – our experiences need to be relevant.

- Manageable – having the necessary tools to manage our experiences.

This is another way of saying that every individual, autistic and non-autistic alike, strives for a healthy balance between understanding, experiencing, and action. Balance in these three areas leads to healthy experiences and interactions.

Sensory integration and coordination: sensory integration is the goal of integrating our sensory experiences, but for the autistic person it is often more important to coordinate the sensory experiences. It might be very difficult to achieve sensory integration with many sensory channels being activated simultaneously, but sensory coordination through choosing which aspects of a sensory experience to relate to at any given time allows the autistic individual some measure of control over their experience and validates their autistic subjectivity. Sensory coordination also allows for a higher degree of access to the executive functions, and ultimately the autistic person becomes more socially functional.

References

Antonovsky, A. (1987) *Unraveling The Mystery of Health – How People Manage Stress and Stay Well.* San Francisco, CA: Jossey-Bass Publishers.

APA (American Psychiatric Association) (2013) *Diagnostic and Statistical Manual of Mental Disorders: DSM-5.* Washington, DC: APA.

Baron-Cohen, S. (1997) *Mindblindness – An Essay on Autism and Theory of Mind.* A Bradford Book. Cambridge, MA: MIT Press.

Moraine, P. (2012) *Helping Students Take Control of Everyday Executive Functions – The Attention Fix.* London and Philadelphia, PA: Jessica Kingsley Publishers.

Palmer, P. (2007) *The Courage to Teach* (10th edition). San Francisco, CA: Jossey-Bass.

Vermeulen, P. (2011) "Autism: From mind blindness to context blindness." *Autism Asperger's Digest,* Nov/Dec. Available from http://autismdigest.com/context-blindness.

Index